KU-669-968
WITHDRAWN

WP 0170327 7
294.60954/MAC

THE EVOLUTION OF THE SIKH COMMUNITY

THE EVOLUTION OF THE SIKH COMMUNITY

Five Essays

W. H. McLEOD

CLARENDON PRESS · OXFORD
1976

Oxford University Press, Ely House, London W. 1

GLASGOW NEW YORK TORONTO MELBOURNE WELLINGTON
CAPE TOWN IBADAN NAIROBI DAR ES SALAAM LUSAKA ADDIS ABABA
DELHI BOMBAY CALCUTTA MADRAS KARACHI LAHORE DACCA
KUALA LUMPUR SINGAPORE HONG KONG TOKYO

ISBN 0 19 826529 8

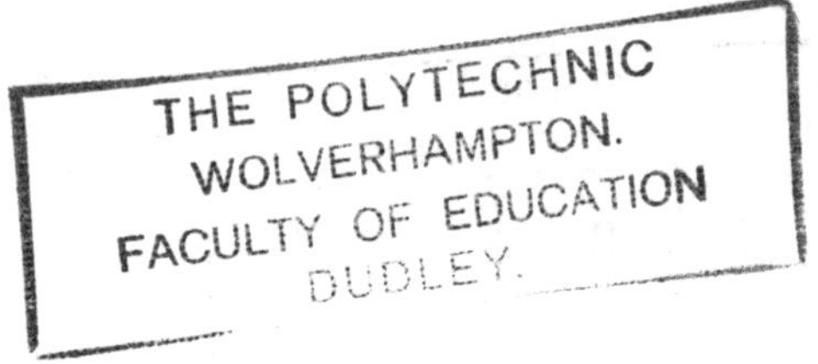

Set in India by
Eastend Printers, Calcutta
Printed in Great Britain by
William Clowes & Sons, Limited
London, Beccles and Colchester

To

F.R.A.

ACKNOWLEDGEMENTS

THE essays which together constitute this small book owe their origin to a series of four lectures delivered in the University of Cambridge during the Lent Term of 1970 under the auspices of the Faculty of Oriental Studies. The first four essays represent revised versions of these lectures. To the Dean of the Faculty, Professor John Emerton, and to all its members I offer my sincere thanks for the invitation which prompted the lectures and for the many kindnesses which I received during a pleasant year in their midst.

I must also record with deep appreciation the fact that the year in Cambridge was made possible by a generous grant from the Managers of the Smuts Memorial Fund. During the course of the year I discovered, to my great pleasure and advantage, the degree to which the Managers, individually as well as collectively, take a genuine and practical interest in their beneficiaries. With much gratitude I acknowledge the assistance which I received during the term of my fellowship from Professor E. E. Rich and his Committee. I also extend my grateful thanks to the Provost and Fellows of King's College for their generous hospitality during my year in Cambridge.

Several persons have aided either the original preparation of the lectures or their subsequent revision. One to whom I owe a special debt for this and much more besides is Dr. F. R. Allchin of Churchill College, Cambridge. Others who have rendered valuable assistance are Mr. Ben Farmer, Dr. Ganda Singh, Professor J. S. Grewal, Professor Harbans Singh, Dr. Stuart McGregor, Dr. Joyce Pettigrew, Mr. G. S. Rahi, Dr. Satish Saberwal, Professor E. Shils, Dr. Percival Spear, and Professor Peter Wilson. I thank them all, and in fairness to them hasten to add that for all opinions and conclusions expressed in these essays I alone am to be held responsible. This vicarious disclaimer must be stressed as the essays incorporate interpretations from which some of my friends and helpers would assuredly wish to dissociate themselves.

Thanks are also due to Professor Fauja Singh of the Department of Punjab Historical Studies at Punjabi University, Patiala, for permission to include in the second essay material previously used for a paper read at the 1969 session of the Punjab History Conference, and to Miss Irene Marshall for typing the entire work. And as always I owe to my wife gratitude beyond expressing for all her sympathy and help.

Finally I must thank my Sikh friends in the Pañjāb for the patience and tolerance which they have so graciously shown towards an interfering foreigner. I am acutely aware that some of the opinions expressed in this book will impose a measure of strain upon their tolerance. This is commonly the case when deeply held convictions are subjected to academic scrutiny and I am bound to recognize that my small volume will be no exception. In conversation with Sikh friends I have frequently referred to 'a concern for sympathetic understanding'. This concern continues undiminished and it is in this spirit that I offer these five essays to them.

The University of Otago,
Dunedin

Hew McLeod

CONTENTS

1. The Evolution of Sikh Community 1

2. The Janam-sākhīs 20

3. Cohesive Ideals and Institutions in the History of the Sikh Panth 37

4. The Sikh Scriptures 59

5. Caste in the Sikh Panth 83

GLOSSARY 105

BIBLIOGRAPHY 111

INDEX 115

I

THE EVOLUTION OF THE SIKH COMMUNITY

TRAVELLING into New Delhi from Palam airport one is likely to find that the taxi is being driven by a Sikh. This will at once be evident from the driver's beard and distinctive turban. A prolonged stay in India will soon supplement this initial observation with a wider range of impressions concerning the Sikh people, impressions which in addition to the beards, turbans, and taxis will probably accommodate a reputation for physical prowess and a fund of mildly insulting jokes. This is the current stereotype. It suggests a community easily defined, one with well-marked bounds and an essentially homogeneous constituency. The available literature does much to encourage this impression and extends the same assurance to cover the period of historical development which produced the contemporary community. A superficial survey of this literature might well suggest that the pattern of Sikh history, like its contemporary expression, is simple and straightforward.

These impressions should be dispelled, for they misrepresent both the pattern of Sikh history and the nature of modern Sikh society. Historical antecedents and contemporary realities are both much more complex than the stereotype would suggest. This, surely, is to be expected. A community which in its contemporary form is constituted by a variety of cultural influences and by an eventful history of more than four hundred years is not to be summed up in terms of simple generalizations. These must be unravelled and examined. Only when we reach some understanding of those diverse cultural influences and obscure historical processes can we lay claim to any real understanding of the contemporary community.

A quest of this nature is well worth the labour which it involves. The Sikhs are an unusually interesting people, an extremely capable community which exercises upon the life of modern India an influence far greater than its numerical strength might otherwise warrant. To appreciate their importance one need look no further than Indian sport, political activity, and the armed services. Moreover, the community's impact is now to be felt in areas beyond the boundaries of India, a fact to which certain transport committees in the United Kingdom will bear testimony.[1] The record is an impressive one and it is matched by the considerable interest which attaches to the community's past. Sikh history presents us with a problem at once fascinating and perplexing. Those four and a half centuries of Sikh history offer an unusually coherent example of how a cultural group develops in direct response to the pressure of historical circumstances. The attempt to trace that history in detail must, however, encounter difficulties. The general outline may be clear but there are some blank patches, tantalizing gaps which in the condition of existing knowledge we can fill only by recourse to conjecture.

Before any attempt is made to trace this outline an important word must be introduced and defined. Up to this point the collective term used to designate the Sikh people has been the word 'community'. Conventional English usage sanctions the term and for this reason it appears in the title of this work. There are, however, disadvantages in continuing to use it. Within India the term has been sullied by association with the less admirable aspects of communalism, with the result that it no longer retains its neutral meaning when used in a specifically religious context. Moreover, by abandoning the word in this context we free it for a more convenient usage in a different context. For references to the religious community of the Sikhs the term normally used will hereafter be the word Panth (*panth*, literally 'path' or 'road' but customarily used with reference to particular systems of religious belief). The Sikhs themselves habitually refer to their own community as the Panth, and within the Pañjāb the word is so widely understood that it regularly appears in the English-language press without gloss or translation.[2] Deprived of this usage the word

[1] David Bentham, *Transport and Turbans: A Comparative Study in Local Politics* (London, 1970).

[2] The adjectival form 'panthic' is also commonly used, as in the expressions 'panthic welfare' or 'panthic unity'. For a discussion of Sikh usage of the term *panth* see J. S. Grewal, *From Guru Nanak to Maharaja Ranjit Singh* (Amritsar, 1972), chap. VI. The pronunciation of *panth* is very similar to the English word 'punt'

'community' can now be employed to designate specific social groups which have contributed to the membership of the Panth.[3]

There is nothing new in the idea that the Sikh Panth as we know it today is the evolved product of a period of many years. This merely states the obvious. In this particular context the concept of evolution, or of transformation, has been universally accepted, and major disagreements have concerned little more than the question of whether or not subsequent developments were in total accord with the teachings of Gurū Nānak. The orthodox Sikh interpretation insists upon the notion of complete accord, not merely with the teachings but also with the actual intention of the first Gurū; whereas some other commentators have suggested radical divergence from those teachings.

According to the generally accepted understanding of Sikh development there have been three major stages in the evolutionary process.[4] The first was the work of Gurū Nānak who is almost invariably referred to as 'the founder of Sikhism'. Gurū Nānak, it is maintained, propounded original teachings, established a new religion, and gathered round himself a following drawn from both Hindus and Muslims. This was the first and basic stage, and it took place during the first half of the sixteenth century.

The second came during the time of Gurū Hargobind, the sixth Gurū, whose period occupies most of the first half of the seventeenth century. Gurū Arjan, the fifth Gurū and father of Hargobind, had in some manner incurred the displeasure of the Mughal authorities and in 1606 had died while in custody. The incident is an obscure one, but later tradition tolerates no doubts. Gurū Arjan's death was, according to this later tradition, the death of a martyr at the hands of Muslims who feared his growing power as a religious leader.

This incident (so the tradition continues) indicated to the Sikhs a manifest intention to put down the developing panth

with the terminal consonant aspirated. The same pronunciation is used for the first syllable of 'panthic'.

[3] As such it will correspond to *zāt* or *jāti*, the endogamous caste grouping. See below, pp. 10, 89.

[4] For a summary statement of this interpretation see Harbans Singh, *The Heritage of the Sikhs* (Bombay, 1964), pp. 19–44. See also Gokul Chand Narang, *The Transformation of Sikhism* (Lahore, 1912 and numerous reprints), pp. 1–87: and Khushwant Singh, *A History of the Sikhs*, Vol. 1 (Princeton, N. J., 1963), pp. 96–8.

and persuaded the sixth Gurū that for the defence of his following he would have to resort to arms. He accordingly responded to the Mughal threat of violent repression by arming his followers and by inculcating martial instincts. Nothing basic had, however, been changed. The religious teachings of Nānak were retained intact, the only difference being that those who practised them would now be prepared to defend by military means their right to do so.

Tradition also attributes the third and final stage to the hostile intentions of the Mughals. This stage was marked by an event which took place on a particular day in the year 1699. The tenth Gurū, Gobind Siṅgh, having observed the growing hostility of both the hill rajas and the Mughal authorities, and having reflected upon the weakness of his own followers, reached a momentous decision. This decision he put into effect during the Baisākhī festival of 1699, and the result was the founding of the Khālsā.

The Khālsā is best described as an order, as a society possessing a religious foundation and a military discipline. The religious base was already in existence and a military tradition had been developed, but something much stronger was required. The military aspect had to be fused with the religious, and this Gurū Gobind Siṅgh achieved by promulgating the Order of the Khālsā on that fateful day in 1699. Thus were the sparrows transformed into hawks. Thus was there forged first in the mind of Gurū Gobind Siṅgh and then within the corporate body of his followers a community dedicated to the defence of righteousness by the use of the sword, an invincible army of saint-soldiers destined to withstand the most fearsome of persecutions, destined to overthrow the evil power of the Mughals, destined ultimately to usher in, under Mahārājā Rañjīt Siṅgh, the most glorious period in the history of the Pañjāb.

This, then, is the tradition—a theory of evolution in three stages which with greater or less sophistication still commands almost universal acceptance. It is, however, an interpretation which must be considerably modified. This insistence should not imply that the concept of development is to be discarded, nor is there any intention of disputing the importance of the three accepted stages. The purpose of this essay is to seek a more radical concept of development, one which will express a much more intricate synthesis of a much wider range of historical and sociological phenomena. Our basic disagreement with the traditional interpretation concerns its simplicity. It starts too late and ends too soon. It omits vital elements within the limited area which it claims to cover. It over-simplifies the events to which it does attribute importance and lays upon them a weight of emphasis which in all three cases is considerably in excess of their true significance.

Let us first consider the position of Gurū Nānak within this pattern. Gurū Nānak was born in the Pañjāb in 1469, travelled extensively in India as a religious pilgrim, and died in the Pañjāb in 1539. During the latter years of his lifetime he gathered a group of followers to whom the title 'Sikh' or 'disciple' came to be applied. This group constituted the original *Nānak-panth*, the religious following which was to develop into the Sikh Panth of today.

To Sikhs of all subsequent generations Gurū Nānak is the founder of the Sikh religion. Of his importance there can be no doubt whatsoever, and it must also be acknowledged that in a certain sense he is legitimately described as a founder. The following which gathered around this man was certainly the original nucleus of the Sikh Panth and if we are to follow organizational lines in our movement back through history we shall be able to proceed no further than this nucleus and this man.

In another sense, however, the term 'founder' is misleading, for it suggests that Gurū Nānak originated not merely a group of followers but also a school of thought, or set of teachings. This can be accepted as true only in a highly qualified sense. If we place Gurū Nānak within his own historical context, if we compare his teachings with those of other contemporary or earlier religious figures, we shall at once see that he stands firmly within a well-defined tradition. What Gurū Nānak offers us is the clearest and most highly articulated expression of the *nirguṇa sampradāya*, the so-called Sant tradition of Northern India.

Having recognized this affiliation we are also compelled to recognize that our search for the evolutionary pattern must take us back beyond the time and the teachings of Gurū Nānak. It must first take us to the earlier representatives of the Sant tradition, and then as we trace out the antecedents of their thought we soon find ourselves following those endless paths which eventually disappear in the mists of India's antiquity.

The school of thought which we call the Sant tradition of Northern India is commonly confused with that vast area of medieval devotion which is popularly referred to as the Bhakti Movement, or with the Vaiṣṇava expression of that movement.[5] Kabīr, the greatest of the Sants before Nānak, is normally regarded as one among many devotional poets of medieval India. It is true that Vaiṣṇava bhakti constituted a primary element of the Sant synthesis, but it was an element which had been largely transformed by its association with another important element. This second element was the doctrine of the Nāth tradition. The Nāth tradition was, in later medieval times, the most important expression of the ancient tantric tradition. Its exponents were yogīs who claimed to be followers of Gorakhnāth, and their distinctive discipline embodied the practice of haṭha-yoga. They are variously referred to as Nāths, as Gorakhnāthīs, and as Kānphaṭ or 'split-ear' yogīs, the latter designation arising from their custom of piercing the ears and inserting large ear-rings.

Haṭha-yoga affirms in an absolute sense a doctrine of interiority and finds its ultimate expression in an ineffable experience of mystical unity at the climax of a psycho-physical ascent within the human body. This absolute insistence upon the interior nature of their discipline inevitably involved the Nāths in a total rejection of all such external elements as idols, ritual, temples and mosques, pilgrimage and caste. They were also distinguished by their usage of vernacular languages.

It was the influence of Nāth doctrine and practice upon Vaiṣṇava bhakti which was primarily responsible for the emergence of the Sant synthesis. Muslim beliefs, both Sūfī and orthodox, had at most a marginal effect. The Vaiṣṇava insistence upon loving adoration remains central, but the understanding of the nature of this adoration has been transformed by Nāth concepts of unity, interiority, and the mystical ascent. In Kabīr we find a doctrine of unmediated interior devotion

[5] For the Sant tradition of Northern India see the introductions to Charlotte Vaudeville's *Kabīr*, Vol. 1 (Oxford, 1974), *Au cabaret de l'amour* (Paris, 1959), and *Kabīr Granthāvalī* (*Dohā*) (Pondichery, 1957). See also W. H. McLeod, *Gurū Nānak and the Sikh Religion* (Oxford, 1968), pp. 151–8.

directed to a formless, immanent, non-incarnated God. All external practices are spurned, and the sundering of the bond of transmigration is found in mystical union with God.

This is precisely the doctrine which we find in the works of Gurū Nānak. There is no strong evidence to suggest that Nānak knew of Kabīr, but there can be no doubt that both stand within the same tradition and that they share it with many lesser figures. Although the teachings of Gurū Nānak do indeed constitute a synthesis it is not that synthesis of 'Hinduism and Islam' which finds mention in most surveys of his thought. It is the Sant synthesis, a system which he inherited, reworked according to his own genius, and passed on in a form unequalled by any other representative of the tradition. The greatness of Gurū Nānak lay in his capacity to integrate a somewhat disparate set of doctrines, and to express them with clarity and a compelling beauty. Salvation for Gurū Nānak lay in interior meditation upon the divine Name, upon all that constitutes the divine Presence. Others accepted the teaching as valid and the teacher as inspired. In this manner the Sikh Panth was born.

Following the death of Gurū Nānak in 1539 the leadership of the Panth passed to a chosen disciple named Aṅgad.[6] Of Gurū Aṅgad's period we know very little that can be accepted with anything approaching assurance and we can only assume that the constituency and discipline of the Panth must have followed the pattern established under Nānak. With the third Gurū, however, we come to clear indications of one significant change, and to strong hints of another important development.

Gurū Amar Dās, who succeeded Gurū Aṅgad in 1552, lived in Goindvāl, at that time an important town on the imperial high road and on the right bank of the Beās river. If one visits Goindvāl today one will find there a *bāolī*, a large well with steps leading down to it. One may also observe that the steps

[6] The principal source used by most modern writers for the life of Gurū Aṅgad and for much of the subsequent Gurū period is Santokh Singh's *Gur Pratāp Sūray*, popularly known as the *Sūraj Prakāś*. This substantial work was completed in A.D. 1844, a date which at once indicates the risks involved in relying upon it (or upon the same author's earlier *Nānak Prakāś*) for authentic information concerning the period of the Gurūs. Santokh Singh was a hagiographer and as such produced works of considerable importance for an understanding of Sikh history during the early nineteenth century. His works cannot, however, be regarded as reliable sources for the period which they purport to cover and can be used for this purpose only with extreme caution.

number eighty-four. Tradition ascribes the original digging of this well to the command of Gurū Amar Dās and there is every reason to accept this particular tradition as accurate. The significance of the well lies in its relation to the teachings of Gurū Nānak on the one hand; and to other such watering-places on the other. The intention of Gurū Amar Dās, according to the tradition, was that this well should be the Sikhs' *tīrath*, or centre of pilgrimage, and certainly the eighty-four steps (corresponding to the traditional eighty-four lakhs of existences in the total transmigratory cycle) suggest that the purpose of the well was more than the mere provision of drinking-water.

If we set this new well against the teachings of Gurū Nānak we find an apparent contradiction. Gurū Nānak, with all the characteristic Sant emphasis upon interiority, had declared in very plain terms that there was only one *tīrath*, only one pilgrimage-centre for the true devotee, and that was within his own heart.[7] All others were useless. Here, however, we find his second successor apparently inaugurating the very thing he had spurned. Obviously we have in the establishment of this new pilgrimage-centre the response of a leader who is facing problems of definition and of organization. Such problems would have been slight in the early days, but now the Panth is growing. A second generation is coming up and the bond of immediate personal commitment is weakening. Bonds other than those based upon religious belief are becoming necessary and the third Gurū finds the solution in recourse to traditional Indian institutions. Not only did he provide this new pilgrimage-centre, but also distinctive festival-days, distinctive rituals, and a collection of sacred writings. Gurū Nānak had rejected all of these. Gurū Amar Dās, in different and more difficult circumstances, is compelled to return to them.

Change is accordingly taking place, but it should be stressed that the change is not yet radical. Two qualifications must be added. The first is that the developments which appeared during the period of Gurū Amar Dās should not be interpreted as a rejection of Gurū Nānak's primary emphasis upon interior devotion. The words of Gurū Amar Dās are in accord with those of the first Gurū, and the doctrinal lines laid down by Nānak are continued by his second successor. The innovations

[7] *Japjī* 21 (*Ādi Granth*, p. 4). W. H. McLeod, op. cit., pp. 210–11, 213.

introduced by Gurū Amar Dās must be seen as concessions to social needs, not as a conscious shift in doctrine.

Secondly, the innovations which Gurū Amar Dās evidently introduced were not really innovations at all, for he did little more than reintroduce traditional Hindu customs. There is, however, a strong element of distinction. The pilgrimage-centre is in Goindvāl. It is not at Hardwar, nor at Kurukshetra, nor at any of the other places which his followers might have visited. The Sikh Panth is developing a consciousness of its own separate nature. Links with Hindu tradition are very clear but so too is the intention to draw lines which will imply distinction. The point should not, however, be emphasized too strongly. Throughout Sikh history there has been constant movement into and out of the Panth along caste lines, and there have always existed many families whose allegiance to the community has been only partial. In such cases all members of the family do not own an explicit adherence to Sikh belief and practice. For a Pañjābī family of today this will mean that at least one member accepts the discipline in its entirety. Of the remainder some will claim doctrinal belief without formal observance of the discipline, and others will call themselves Hindus.

A second important development which appears to have been taking place during the period of Gurū Amar Dās concerns the constitution of the rising Panth. All ten Gurūs came from Khatrī families and there are other indications that the Khatrīs commanded a particular influence within the Panth during its early years. From the very beginning, however, many Jaṭs were attracted to the Gurū's following and it seems that by the time of the third Gurū their numbers within the Panth must have been increasing faster than those of any other caste group. It is true that the pattern is still in some measure unclear and that we may perhaps be pushing the significant growth of Jaṭ allegiance too far back in time. The dwelling-places of the first three Gurūs suggest, however, that the movement must have been under way by this time. All three lived within, or very close to, the Mājhā, an area in central Pañjāb which possessed and possesses a particularly high proportion of Jaṭs. Even if we allow a measure of doubt as far as this earliest period is concerned it is clear that the movement was certainly taking place by the time of the fifth Gurū, Arjan, whose period extended from 1581 to 1606. The founding of the villages of Tarn Tāran, Srī Hargobindpur, and Kartārpur (all of them in Jaṭ territory) puts this beyond doubt.[8]

To appreciate the meaning of this development it is obviously necessary to understand something of the contrasting features of Khatrī and Jaṭ society. In order to avoid using the misleading term 'caste' we shall here describe both the Khatrīs and the Jaṭs as communities, a word which was earlier deprived of its narrowly religious connotation that it might serve this purpose. The Khatrīs may be defined as an urban-based mercantile community, some of whose members are to be found living in villages. Trade has been their distinctive occupation, although many are to be found in administration, clerical employment, and industry. In contrast, the Jaṭs are a rural and agrarian community consisting largely of peasants and landlords. Although the two communities belong primarily to the Pañjāb representatives of both have migrated elsewhere in India and overseas.

The situation which now emerges is that within the Sikh Panth leadership drawn from a mercantile community secures a substantial and increasing following drawn from an agrarian community. This Jaṭ incursion was of considerable importance in the evolution of the Panth, particularly for the developments which took place during the seventeenth and eighteenth centuries. Even today a substantial majority of Sikhs are Jaṭs.[9] During the seventeenth and eighteenth centuries, prior to the admission of large numbers of Aroṛās and outcaste groups, their influence must have been even stronger. Although the respect accorded to Khatrīs obviously continued, the Jaṭ constituency was preponderant and the inevitable result was development along lines dictated by the influence of Jaṭ cultural patterns.

The origins of the Jaṭ community are still disputed, but fortunately we are not here concerned with those origins. The issue which concerns us here is neither the origin of the community, nor the label which we attach to it, but its nature.

[8] Note also the significant reference to Jaṭ influence made during the period of the sixth Gurū by the author of the *Dabistān-i-Mazāhib*. Ganda Singh, English translation in *The Panjab Past and Present*, Vol. 1, Part 1, no. 1, p. 57.

[9] See below, p. 93.

With their strong rural base, their martial traditions, their normally impressive physique, and their considerable energy the Jaṭs have for many centuries constituted the élite of the Pañjāb villages. They are also noted for their straightforward manner, for a tremendous generosity, for an insistence upon the right to take vengeance, and for their sturdy attachment to the land. They have long dominated rural Pañjāb and at certain times their influence has extended much further. Today, with agriculture expanding rapidly in the Pañjāb, they are experiencing another period of resurgence.

Why did the Jaṭs enter this new panth in such large numbers? Their evident willingness to do so was presumably facilitated by the fact that Khatrīs commonly served as teachers of the Jaṭs. Khatrīs could be expected to direct their teachings to Jaṭs, and Jaṭs could be expected to respond. Nānak, the first of the Khatrī line, was an unusually gifted teacher and the reputation earned by the emergent *Nānak-panth* was doubtless strengthened by the notable sanctity of his successors. For such men a sympathetic Jaṭ audience would be assured.

This traditional relationship can be regarded as one reason for Jaṭ accessions to the early Panth. By itself, however, it seems inadequate as a means of explaining the apparent volume of Jaṭ membership. An interesting solution to this problem has been offered by Professor Irfan Habib. The Jaṭs of the Pañjāb can, he suggests, be traced to a pastoral people of the same name who appear in reports dating from the period between the seventh and ninth centuries and who were distinguished by a notable absence of social or economic stratification. From Sind this Jaṭ people moved northwards via Multān into the Pañjāb and eastwards across the Jamnā River. In the course of their migration they changed from pastoralists to peasant cultivators. They thus advanced economically while retaining the social stigma attached to their earlier pastoral status. This widening disparity, fortified by their inherited egalitarian traditions, attracted them to a line of Gurūs who rejected the theory of caste and willingly raised Jaṭs to positions of high authority in the new Panth.[10]

The theory is an attractive one. Certainly there seems to be

[10] Irfan Habib, *Proceedings of the Punjab History Conference 1971* (Patiala, 1972), pp. 49–54 *passim.*

little doubt that in some sense the egalitarian emphasis of the Gurūs' teachings must be regarded as a primary reason for the extensive Jaṭ allegiance to the Panth. Whatever the reason, it is clear that many Jaṭs of the central Pañjāb did become Sikhs and that the Sikh Panth was deeply affected by its Jaṭ constituency. Inevitably it became in many respects a reflection of Jaṭ cultural patterns, adding to the interior devotion of Nānak features derived from their distinctive customs and values. It is in the light of this process that we must view the second stage of the traditional three-tier pattern of development.

This second stage concerns the conflict between the Sikhs and the Mughal authorities during the early seventeenth century. Tradition, as we have already seen, attributes the genesis of this conflict to Mughal fears concerning the growing power of the Sikh Gurū, and interprets the militant posture of Gurū Hargobind as a direct response to Mughal threats. There can be no doubt that Mughal hostility was developing during this period, but we must beware of attributing it solely to Jahāngīr's orthodoxy or to the promptings of his Naqshbandī courtiers. The increasing influence of the Jaṭs within the Sikh Panth suggests that Jahāngīr and his subordinates may well have had good reason for their fears, and that these fears would not have related exclusively, nor even primarily, to the *religious* influence of the Gurū.

It also suggests that the arming of the Panth would not have been the result of any decision by Gurū Hargobind. We may be sure that the Jaṭs did not enter the Panth empty-handed. They would have been bearing arms many years before Gurū Arjan died in Lahore. The death of Gurū Arjan may have persuaded Gurū Hargobind of the need for tighter organization, but we find it difficult to envisage a large group of unarmed Jaṭs suddenly being commanded to take up weapons. The Jaṭs will have remained Jaṭs. The development which tradition ascribes to a decision by Gurū Hargobind must have preceded, and in some measure prompted, the first Mughal efforts to curb the growing power of the community. The conflict with the Mughals certainly exercised a most important influence upon the subsequent development of the Panth, but not an influence of the kind attributed to it by Sikh tradition. The growth of militancy within the Panth must be traced primarily to the impact of Jaṭ cultural patterns and to economic problems which prompted a militant response.

There was, however, one important decision which Gurū Hargobind took in response to Mughal hostility. This was the decision to leave the plains and move to the Śivālik Hills, the low range which separates the plains of the Pañjāb from the Himālayas. This move took place in the year 1634 when the Gurū retired to the village of Kīratpur. From this time onwards Gurū Hargobind and all four of his successors spent most of their time in the Śivālik Hills. It was in these hills that the tenth Gurū was brought up, and for most of his period as Gurū he was exclusively occupied in Śivālik affairs. Only towards the end did a Mughal force from Sirhind enter what was essentially a Śivālik Hills war.

Why is this emphasis upon the Śivāliks so important? Its importance lies in the fact that the Śivālik Hills have long been a stronghold of the Devī or Śakti cult.[11] A journey from Ambālā up through the Śivāliks to Śimlā will, if one observes the place-names along the way, bear testimony to this fact. Ambālā itself is one such instance, Chaṇḍīgaṛh is the next, and Kalkā a third. The hills of the Pañjāb are culturally distinct from the plains and one of the most prominent instances of this difference is to be found in the Śakti aspects of the hills culture.

The result of prolonged residence within the Śivāliks was that elements of the hills culture eventually penetrated the Jaṭ Sikh culture of the plains and produced yet another stage in the evolution of the Panth. It is in the works of Gurū Gobind Siṅgh and in the developments which followed his death that we can observe this influence most plainly. God, for Gurū Gobind Siṅgh, was personified by steel and worshipped in the form of the sword. For him the characteristic name of God was *sarab-loh*, the 'All-Steel', and it is no accident that in the preparation for Sikh baptism the baptismal water is stirred with a two-edged sword. In his writings and in those which were produced at his court we find constant references to the mighty exploits of the Mother Goddess, one of the most notable being his own *Chaṇḍī kī Vār*.

[11] *śakti*, 'power', the active power of a male deity personified by his female consort. As a cultic term Śakti refers to the worship of Devī the Mother Goddess, consort of Śiva and variously manifested as Pārvatī, Kālī, and Durgā. I owe this hypothesis to Dr. Niharranjan Ray.

The source of these new emphases is quite clear. Obviously they are derived from the Śakti elements of the Śivālik Hills culture. The developments which took place within the Panth during this period cannot be explained without some reference to the *Mārkaṇḍeya Purāṇa* and to the beliefs which it so vividly expresses. This Śakti blended easily with the Jaṭ cultural patterns which had been brought from the plains. The result was a new and powerful synthesis, one which prepared the Panth for a determinative role in the chaotic circumstances of the eighteenth century.

We come now to that turbulent century, or rather to the year which stood at its very threshold. The year 1699 is, without doubt, the high point of Sikh tradition. According to this tradition all that had preceded 1699 was a preparation for the mighty climax which it produced; and all that follows has been the application and the product of that climax. The climax to which we refer was the founding of the Khālsā Brotherhood on the Baisākhī festival day of 1699.

What actually happened on that momentous day? Let us look first at the testimony of Sikh tradition, endeavouring as far as possible to preserve the spirit as well as the content of that tradition. It is believed that Gurū Gobind Siṅgh, having reflected upon the perils of his situation and the apparent weakness of his timid followers, had devised a plan whereby to infuse a spirit of strength and unity. This plan he put into effect on that Baisākhī day. Summoned from far and wide, his followers had gathered in their thousands at Anandpur Sāhib. The Gurū had, however, concealed himself in a tent which had been erected on the fair-ground. There he remained in seclusion until the fair was in full swing, when suddenly he emerged before his followers. With fearsome countenance and sword raised aloft he demanded the head of any one of his Sikhs.

A hush fell upon the mighty concourse and the Gurū repeated his demand. Eventually a loyal Sikh came forward and was conducted to the tent. Those who remained outside heard the thud of a descending sword and observed with horror that the Gurū, when he reappeared, bore a blood-stained weapon. Their horror increased when he demanded a second head, and when another Sikh came forward the same process was repeated. Eventually five such volunteers were escorted into the tent. When the Gurū reappeared after dispatching his fifth victim he proceeded to draw back the side of the tent. Horror changed to amazement when the gathering observed the five supposed victims alive and well. Beside them lay the corpses of five decapitated goats.

The Gurū then delivered a sermon. The five who had in loyalty to him volunteered their lives were, he declared, to constitute the nucleus of a new brotherhood, the Khālsā. Those who chose to enlist in this brotherhood were to abandon pride of caste; they were to abandon the old scriptures and places of pilgrimage; and they were to abandon the worship of minor gods, goddesses, and *avatārs*. Instead they were to follow only God and the Gurū.

Next the Gurū prepared *amrit*, or 'nectar', for a baptismal ceremony. Sweets were mingled with water in an iron bowl and stirred with a two-edged sword. The preparation was administered to the five foundation members who were then instructed to administer the same baptism to the Gurū himself. After this all who were willing to join the brotherhood and to accept its discipline were invited to take baptism, and it is said that many thousands of all castes came forward.

Finally the discipline was promulgated. Five groups of people were to be avoided, all of them either the followers of relatives who had at various times disputed the succession to the Gurū-ship, or else cutters of hair. Various prohibitions were enjoined, notably tobacco, meat from animals slaughtered in the Muslim fashion, and sexual intercourse with Muslim women. And five symbols were to be worn. These were the 'Five K's' (uncut hair, a comb, a steel bangle, a dagger, and a particular variety of breeches). All men who joined the brotherhood were to add the name Siṅgh, or 'Lion', to their given name, and all women were to add Kaur.

Thus was the Khālsā Brotherhood founded. An idea was born in the mind of the tenth Gurū and put into effect on that fateful Baisākhī day. A powerful brotherhood was established, one which in unity, loyalty, and courage was to struggle against overwhelming odds, survive the cruellest of persecution, and ultimately rise to supremacy on the ruins of Mughal power and Afghān pretensions. To this event we must add one more to complete the tradition concerning the birth of the Khālsā. It is believed that shortly before his death in 1708 Gurū Gobind Siṅgh declared the line of personal Gurūs to be at an end. Following his death the functions of the Gurū were to vest jointly in the body of believers (the *Khālsā Panth*) and the scripture (the *Granth Sāhib*).[12]

This is the traditional interpretation of the founding of the Khālsā. It leads us into the eighteenth century, for our understanding of these traditions must be evaluated in the light of what we find in the period extending from the institution of the Khālsā in 1699 to the capture of Lahore by Rañjīt Siṅgh in 1799. We must at once own that our knowledge of this century is still limited. Traditions abound but so too do compulsive reasons for scepticism. What we do know, however, indicates that the traditions relating to the period of Gurū Gobind Siṅgh must be, in some considerable measure, set aside. The slate must be wiped clean and must not be reinscribed until we have ascertained just what did take place during the eighteenth century, We may be sure that something certainly did happen on that Baisākhī day of 1699, and that some of the traditions will eventually turn out to be substantially accurate. Moreover, there can be no doubt that the Khālsā did eventually establish an effectual claim to represent the orthodox form of the Sikh Panth. Already, however, it is possible to demonstrate that many of the traditions are historiographical phenomena, features which developed subsequently but which came, in even later interpretations, to be related to the time and intention of Gurū Gobind Siṅgh.[13]

The eighteenth century was, even for the Pañjāb, an unusually disturbed period.[14] Immediately after the death of Gurū Gobind Siṅgh there followed a peasant revolt led by the Gurū's follower, Bandā. At one stage during this revolt Mughal authority was almost completely obliterated in the Pañjāb and

[12] Similar accounts of the founding of the Khālsā and of the termination of the line of personal Gurūs will be found in almost every modern work dealing with the period of Gurū Gobind Siṅgh. For examples see M. A. Macauliffe, *The Sikh Religion*, Vol. 5 (Oxford, 1909), pp. 84–97; Teja Singh and Ganda Singh, *A Short History of the Sikhs* (Bombay, 1950), pp. 68–72; Khushwant Singh, op. cit., Vol. 1, pp. 82–6.

[13] On the problem of what actually happened in 1699 see J. S. Grewal, *From Guru Nanak to Maharaja Ranjit Singh* (Amritsar, 1972), chap. IX.

[14] For a narrative account of Sikh history during the eighteenth century see Khushwant Singh, op. cit., Vol. 1, pp. 101–84.

it was not until the capture of Bandā in 1715 that the revolt was finally crushed. The execution of Bandā was succeeded by a period in which the restored Mughal authorities sought to strengthen their ascendancy over the scattered Sikhs, a period which in Sikh tradition is represented as an effort by the Mughals to exterminate the Panth completely. In 1738, however, Nādir Shāh invaded the area and dealt a severe blow to the Mughal restoration. After Nādir Shāh came the series of Afghān invasions led by Ahmad Shāh Abdālī, a catastrophe which by 1753 had brought the final collapse of Mughal power in the Pañjāb.

Ahmad Shāh Abdālī continued to invade the Pañjāb after 1753, but during the later invasions his chief opponents were the Marāṭhās and the Sikhs. During the Battle of Pānīpat in 1761 the Sikhs stood aside to watch the Afghāns and Marāṭhās destroy each other's hopes of dominance, and then taking advantage of this mutual destruction soon established their own supremacy. At first they were divided into a number of highly mobile bands called *misls*. These groups were loosely united by the ties of community, occupation, and religion in the Dal Khālsā, but in essence they were independent and following the final demolition of the Afghān threat they soon fell to fighting each other. Eventually, at the very end of the century, one of the misls secured a total ascendancy over all the others and the chaos of the misl period was followed by four decades of strong, centralized administration. The misl was the Śukerchakiā misl and its leader was Rañjīt Siṅgh.

The analysis of these eighteenth-century developments must be deferred until the third essay, for many of the more significant features represent efforts to define the nature of the Panth and to maintain its cohesion. There is, for example, the question of authority within the evolving Khālsā. As we have already seen, tradition attributes a definitive answer to Gurū Gobind Siṅgh, one which conferred his personal authority upon the sacred scripture and the corporate panth. This may perhaps be a retrospective interpretation, a tradition which owes its origin not to an actual pronouncement of the Gurū but to an insistent need for maintaining the Panth's cohesion during a later period. In the third essay an attempt will be made to explain the historical circumstances which stimulated this theory of dual authority within the Khālsā, and also to show how subsequent developments caused one part of the twofold authority to atrophy.

The highly interesting question of how the distinctive Khālsā discipline evolved also owes its development primarily to the need for panthic cohesion and must likewise be deferred until the third essay. The only point which requires emphasis at this stage is the fact that the Khālsā code of discipline is, like the Khālsā theory of authority, an evolved and evolving product. Although the actual institution of the code may be safely attached to a declaration made by the tenth Gurū in 1699 any analysis of its actual contents must extend over a much wider period. It must relate to cultural features which were already present within Sikh society at that time, and to events which came later, particularly to events which took place during the eighteenth century.

These two issues have been briefly noted both because they have been of fundamental importance in the evolution of the Panth and because they offer us the greatest scope for informed conjecture at the present stage. If we are to acquire an understanding of developments within the Panth during the course of the eighteenth century, then clearly we must devote considerable attention to these two basic questions. Other issues which must obviously have been of major importance are still too obscure to permit any but the most tentative of theories. There is, for example, the question of leadership patterns within the fragmented groups which constituted Sikh society throughout the greater part of the century. Although Khatrī Sikhs must have retained much of their authority within the religious congregations (*saṅgat*) these groups were no longer the sole representatives of the corporate Panth. The dynamic groups are the military jathās and the misls. In spite of their prominence in eighteenth-century Pañjāb history these military bands are still very imperfectly understood. It is obvious that their leadership was largely in Jaṭ hands and eventually it was a Jaṭ misldār, Rañjīt Siṅgh, who secured total ascendancy. Individual chieftains such as Jassā Siṅgh Kalāl (later known as Jassā Siṅgh Ahlūwālīā) and his namesake Jassā Siṅgh Rāmgaṛhiā represent leadership derived from lower-status groups, but do not disturb the dominant pattern. The Jaṭs are a pragmatic people, respecting good military leadership, and willing if necessary to co-operate with other rural communities. There are, however, many questions which remain unanswered. The framework of understanding which can be constructed in this manner is still little more than an outline.[15]

Another obscure topic concerns the impact of agrarian issues upon the course of eighteenth-century Pañjāb history in general and the Panth in particular. It seems clear that the rebellion associated with the name of Bandā was in some measure an agrarian uprising and we are also aware of the fact that the misl system was intimately related to rural society and its economy. But in precisely what manner? And what developments issued from such relations? The topic bristles with question-marks and other important issues offer a similar aspect.

It is indeed a tantalizing prospect which the eighteenth-century history of the Pañjāb offers us. At its conclusion we find a clearly defined Khālsā Panth with formulated religious doctrines, a coherent code of discipline, and the strong conviction that it has been born to rule. To explain the creation of this Panth we have an extensive, generally consistent, and almost universally accepted body of tradition. Confronting this the historian finds in the eighteenth century a period which provides in the midst of a considerable obscurity sufficient indications to call in question much of what has been passed down to us in the tradition. The impression which these glimpses communicate is that of a society in a critical period of evolution. Warfare, disaster, and eventually triumph all bring distinctive problems and distinctive solutions. In both tribulation and success the expanding Panth is ever seeking a self-understanding, a self-definition which in its essentials is maintained to this day. Plainly there can be no hope of comprehending the Sikh Panth of today without a prior understanding of its formative past.

[15] A promising sign of change has been the recent appearance of doctoral theses dealing with this period. Two which deserve special mention are Bhagat Singh, 'Sikh Polity in the Eighteenth and Nineteenth Centuries' (Punjabi University, Patiala, 1971) and Indu Banga, 'The Agrarian System of the Sikhs (1759-1849)' (Guru Nanak University, Amritsar, 1974).

2

THE JANAM-SĀKHĪS

MUCH misunderstanding in the field of Sikh history can be traced directly to the use of sources. The selection has been too narrow and the few which command a particular popularity have sometimes been misinterpreted. This second essay concerns one of the major misinterpretations.

For the period of Sikh history up to the beginning of the nineteenth century there are three main sources. There are the Persian chronicles of the period; the accounts which were written or commissioned by the British in the late eighteenth and early nineteenth centuries; and the corpus of Sikh devotional literature. The first of these tells us little about the Sikhs and not much more about the Pañjāb. With few exceptions the chroniclers were uninterested in the Pañjāb, except when an occasional crisis or royal visit drew their brief attention. The British accounts tell us much more (in most instances their very purpose was, after all, the communication of information concerning the Pañjāb and the Sikhs), but apart from their treatment of the late eighteenth century they are largely unreliable, for they are too far from the events which they purport to describe. This should not imply that these first two groups of sources are valueless. They can be very valuable indeed. Their contributions are, however, fragmentary. None of them contributes a narrative which is at once sustained and reliable.

This leaves us with the devotional literature of the Sikhs. Within this category the obvious work would appear to be the scripture compiled by Gurū Arjan, the *Ādi Granth.* It is, however, a source which is likely to prove something of a disappointment to the historian. For an understanding of later medieval religion it is priceless, but the historian who seeks to use it as a source for a wider knowledge of the culture of the period must work hard for a relatively limited return. A more useful source for this wider understanding is the devotional literature which constitutes the subject of this essay. In this introduction to the janam-sākhīs an attempt will be made to cover three aspects of the literature. First there will be an examination of the nature of the janam-sākhīs and in particular of their development, purpose, and function. This will be followed by a brief analysis of their usefulness as sources for the life of Gurū Nānak. Finally, the essay will conclude with a discussion of their value as sources for the later history of the Sikhs.[1]

A brief etymological excursus will explain the manner in which the term janam-sākhī acquired its present usage. The word *janam* means 'birth', and *sākhī* literally means 'testimony'. In its literal sense the composite term accordingly means a 'birth-testimony'. Originally only the latter term, *sākhī*, appears to have been used. Bābā Nānak was the giver of salvation and the duty of his disciples was to bear witness to this fact. In practice this meant the recitation of anecdotes which in various ways provided evidence in support of the claim. Collections of these anecdotes were soon made and were at first called simply *sākhīān*, or 'testimonies'. Two of these early collections are, however, entitled *janam-patrī*, or 'horoscope'. In a strict sense the title related only to the opening anecdote describing the birth of Nānak and it appears that the term was used in order to impart an impression of authenticity to the complete collection. The two terms both continued to be used and eventually coalesced. The word *patrī* dropped out and the compound *janam-sākhī* survived.

Although janam-sākhīs of other religious figures have since been written the term is generally restricted to collections of anecdotes concerning Gurū Nānak. The usual translation is, as one might expect, 'biography'. This translation is deliberately avoided here for the sufficient reason that the janam-sākhīs are not in fact biographical works. They are strictly hagiographic and only if this is borne in mind can they serve their proper use for the historian. Much misunderstanding has been caused, and continues to be caused, by a widespread acceptance of the janam-sākhīs as biographical, an acceptance which alone makes possible the lengthy accounts of the life and travels of Gurū Nānak which in the wake of his birth quincentenary are enjoying a new lease of life. This acceptance distorts our under-

[1] The janam-sākhīs are more fully discussed in a work at present in preparation, tentatively entitled *Early Sikh Tradition*.

standing of the historical Nānak and (what is equally serious) has led to a total neglect of the true value of the janam-sākhīs. This, as we shall see, consists in the expression which they give to the immensely important Nānak myth of early Sikh tradition,[2] and in their testimony to the period out of which they emerged in their present form, a period which begins almost a century after the death of Nānak.

This gap between the death of Gurū Nānak and the first known recording of janam-sākhī material does not, of course, mean that the literature is totally unrelated to the life of the person whom it purports to describe. The janam-sākhīs as we now possess them have been built upon oral traditions and there is every reason to suppose that these oral traditions must have begun to circulate during the lifetime of the Gurū. One can observe the same process happening today. Holy men flourish in the Pañjāb as much as in any other part of India and one does not have to venture very far into the Pañjāb villages of today to find anecdotes (complete with miracles) of men who are still living.

Oral traditions concerning Gurū Nānak obviously constitute the first stage in the development of the janam-sākhīs. These oral traditions will have sprung from a variety of sources. Some, which we also find related in connection with other celebrated figures, have clearly been borrowed from the common stock of hagiography, and this feature accounts for several of the most popular of all the janam-sākhī episodes. In other cases the source of a borrowing is the common stock of legend. Puranic elements are very prominent in the janam-sākhīs, and Nāth legends also occupy a position of some importance. Other episodes have their origin in some suggestive passage from the Gurū's works. The most obvious illustration of this (and one which at the same time provides an example of Puranic influence) is the discourse on Mount Sumeru with Gorakhnāth and other Masters of the Nāth sect, a story which owes its genesis to a composition in which Gurū Nānak refers to these Nāth Masters by name.[3] And a few must surely have derived from actual incidents in the life of Gurū Nānak, although the prob-

[2] It should be stressed that the word 'myth' is here used in a strictly technical sense and not as a synonym for 'legend'. The issue will be more fully discussed in *Early Sikh Tradition*.

[3] *Ādi Granth*, pp. 952–3.

lem of how to recognize these authentic elements within the mass of legendary material is one of considerable complexity.

These oral traditions will have circulated for many years as isolated stories, or as small clusters. The period of oral circulation prior to the first recording of a selection was evidently lengthy (perhaps as much as a hundred years or more) and it requires little imagination to envisage the extent to which the traditions must have been transmuted as they passed from mouth to mouth. This does not mean, however, that they thereby lost their value for the historian. They lost much of their value as far as our knowledge of the historical Nānak is concerned, but they were always gaining in another sense. The nature of the transformation will have been, in considerable measure, dictated by the situation within which that trasformation took place, and if we can fix any particular janam-sākhī at a point in time we shall have in our possession a most useful means of furthering our understanding of the Sikh Panth at that particular point in time.

After many years of oral transmission the janam-sākhīs moved into a second stage, namely the first recording in written form of portions of the material. A few of the earliest manuscripts indicate that at this stage the various incidents must have been recorded as isolated episodes, the only deference to chronology being a rough grouping according to birth, childhood, manhood, and death. In some cases even this crude structure was evidently lacking.

Chronology characterizes the third stage. Episodes which had previously been related in a disjointed manner are now ordered into a reasonably consistent chronological pattern. Gurū Nānak was known to have travelled extensively. Itineraries are now devised and incidents which already had a particular location are set in appropriate places in the travel narrative. Other incidents which previously had no specific location are now given one. At first the Gurū's travels are relatively modest in extent, but as the years pass from the eighteenth into the nineteenth century we find him reaching Peking in the East and Europe in the West. One relatively recent contribution relates a meeting with the Pope in Rome, an opportunity which Gurū Nānak utilizes to denounce the sale of indulgences.[4]

[4] Lal Singh, *Tavārīkh Gurū Khālsā Panth* (Lahore, 2nd ed., 1945), Vol. 1, p. 140.

A fourth stage is reached when the janam-sākhī material is turned to a different use. Hitherto the emphasis has been upon narrative, and in particular upon the simple wonder-story. Now, in this fourth stage, it moves to exegesis. The various episodes are used as settings for quotations from the Gurū's works, and for lengthy expositions of the passages quoted in this manner. Within the context of a particular incident someone is made to ask a question. In reply the Gurū quotes a verse and the writer adds his own exegesis, normally at some length. This stage bears testimony both to the popularity of the janam-sākhī and to the intelligence of the religious teachers who used it to communicate their message. The people were obviously prepared to listen to janam-sākhīs; the teachers were resourceful enough to recognize this and to make the necessary adaptations.

Most of the janam-sākhīs which we now possess represent either the third or the fourth of these stages, or (more commonly) a combination of the two. They may be divided into a number of groups, or 'traditions', each of which represents the various products of a single source. The most important are the *Purātan* tradition, the *Miharbān* tradition, the *Bālā* tradition, and a version known as the *Ādi Sakhīs*. The janam-sākhīs of the *Purātan* tradition chiefly represent the third stage in the evolutionary pattern (the stage of chronological grouping), but also possess elements of both the second and fourth stages. The *Miharbān* tradition represents the fourth stage; and the *Bālā* a combination of the second and the third, with some elements of the fourth. It should be noted that the age of a tradition is not necessarily reflected in the stage which it represents. The *Bālā* tradition, although predominantly second stage, is actually later than either the *Purātan* janam-sākhīs or the nucleus of the *Miharbān* tradition. All four stages can be found from the early seventeenth century onwards, and all four are still given expression today.

A particular interest attaches, of course, to the seventeenth-century products and perhaps the most interesting of all is the India Office Library manuscript which bears the number *Panjabi B40*. This manuscript, although actually written in the eighteenth century, is essentially a seventeenth-century janam-sākhī in content. It is of particular interest because it best illustrates the second stage, while at the same time offering substantial portions of third-stage and fourth-stage material. Most of this janam-sākhī lacks structure, its individual sākhīs being recorded with little concern for chronology. The first twenty-seven folios are, however, a borrowing from a manuscript shared with the *Purātan* tradition and are related with the characteristic *Purātan* concern for chronological structure. This pattern occasionally recurs, and at other points there intrude exegetical passages which have been taken from a *Miharbān* source.[5]

Ever since the janam-sākhīs first emerged they have enjoyed a considerable popularity. They represent the first Pañjābī prose form, and the dominant prose form up to the emergence of the twentieth-century novel. To this day they retain much of their popularity. They are frequently read in devout Sikh homes and extensively used for instructional purposes in gurdwaras (Sikh temples). This popularity is not difficult to understand. The authors of the janam-sākhīs had developed a considerable narrative power, as a result of which their works make fascinating reading. Their popularity is matched only by their usefulness. To the student of Pañjābī language they are of unusual interest and help in tracing the development of modern Pañjābī prose; and to the historian they are of equal interest and assistance in the quest for an understanding of seventeenth- and eighteenth-century Sikh history.

As we have already observed, the chief use to which the janam-sākhīs have been put by historians of the Pañjāb relates to the life of Gurū Nānak. We have also briefly observed the risks involved in this emphasis, notably the almost universal practice of treating the janam-sākhīs as biographies of Nānak. Having stressed that they are not biographical let us hasten to add that this recognition does not warrant a total rejection of the janam-sākhīs as sources for the life of Nānak. If we reject them we are left with virtually no source for the Gurū's life. It is true, as we have already indicated, that the principal value of the janam-sākhīs relates to a later period, but if carefully scrutinized they can also serve a useful purpose with regard to our knowledge of the historical Nānak.

The basic point which needs to be made as far as the authentic

[5] A complete English translation of the *B40* janam-sākhī will be published separately. All janam-sākhī quotations used in this essay have been taken from this janam-sākhī.

Nānak material is concerned is that the janam-sākhī traditions can provide no more than pointers to possibilities. Each of these possibilities must be subjected to rigorous scrutiny and only when it is actually established can it be accepted. Unlike the prisoner in a court of law the janam-sākhī must be held guilty until proved innocent. A number of tests can be devised in order to test the various episodes in the janam-sākhīs. The incidence of legend is one such test, and a related procedure is the identification of material which has been appropriated from earlier hagiographic traditions. The application of these two obvious criteria will eliminate substantial portions of the janam-sākhī narratives from the authentic Nānak materials. On the other hand it is possible to sustain limited portions by the application of a genealogical criterion. Family memories are long and generally reliable in the Pañjāb, and it is reasonable to assume that when the janam-sākhīs relate details concerning close family relationships they are probably correct. If, of course, the various janam-sākhīs conflict in their testimony to such relationships we must withhold that acceptance, and herein we encounter yet another criterion, namely the measure of agreement or disagreement between the different janam-sākhīs.

The pursuit of this somewhat arduous analysis of the janam-sākhī material will show that most anecdotes are plainly legendary in their application to Gurū Nānak, and it will also establish a few points which withstand all tests. Much will be left between these two definitive extremes and this material we must set aside as unproved. Given the hagiographic nature of the janam-sākhīs and their general lack of reliability as far as the historical Nānak is concerned, material which cannot be positively established should only rarely be given the benefit of the doubt.

If a conviction regarding the unreliability of the janam-sākhīs as biographical records can be communicated it may be possible to develop an understanding of their primary value as historical sources. This primary value concerns the period and the situation out of which the janam-sākhīs emerged. Our earliest recorded janam-sākhīs developed during the early seventeenth century (at least seventy and perhaps as much as one hundred years after the death of Nānak). The seventeenth century was a period of particular popularity, but no generation since then has been without its janam-sākhīs and their importance as contemporary source materials continues to the present day. Once we are in a position to determine the approximate date of a janam-sākhī we shall have in our possession a document which can offer us many insights concerning the beliefs and the environment of the Sikh Panth during that particular period. These insights will chiefly concern the development of the powerful Nānak myth, but their range will extend much further. Inevitably the janam-sākhīs give expression to the wider expanse of Sikh belief and social practice, and at many points their interest passes beyond the confines of the Panth into the rural Pañjāb which was its home.

Let us, in this connection, stress once again the peculiar nature of the janam-sākhīs. The janam-sākhīs are hagiographic, a word which is commonly used in a pejorative sense as a synonym for 'legendary'. Hagiography (like myth) is not properly understood as a synonym for legend, notwithstanding the fact that hagiographic writing characteristically abounds in legendary accounts of mighty deeds. Hagiographic literature is properly understood not as a testimony to popular credulity but rather as a contemporary response to remembered greatness. Upon this memory are focused the needs and the aspirations of a particular group of people at a particular point in time. The treatment accorded to the object of a corporate remembrance will be constituted by a varying blend of authentic memory and subsequent accretion. The accretion must not, however, be dismissed as 'unhistorical'. It may certainly be unhistorical with regard to the person so described, but much of it will be truly historical with regard to the people responsible for the actual expression given to any tradition.

This result follows from the fact that the authors of hagiographic literature must inevitably develop their accounts upon the basis of their own circumscribed understanding. Much will be inherited, but much will derive directly from their own situation. Moreover, the particular expression which they give to their inheritance will draw heavily for its details upon their own experience. When, for example, they deal in any detail with a marriage ceremony they will describe the kind of ceremony which is known to them from their own experience. The janam-sākhī writer Miharbān, when he provides a lengthy account of the marriage of Gurū Nānak, describes not the marriage of Gurū Nānak but a marriage of the kind witnessed by Miharbān himself. The fact that Indian customs change very slowly does indeed mean that Miharbān's account may well be in its essential outline correct, but the principle remains unaltered. We must read this account as a description of a late sixteenth- or early seventeenth-century marriage, not as a late fifteenth-century marriage. As far as the life of Gurū Nānak is concerned it is only the bare statement of the actual event which retains an indisputable validity, namely the statement that he was married in the town of Baṭālā to the daughter of Mūlā Choṇā. This much we can relate to the authentic life of Nānak. The remainder, consisting of all the details which embellish the actual event, we must relate to the period in which the account was actually written.

An issue which serves to illustrate both the connection and the difference between the teachings of the historical Nānak on the one hand and the testimony of the janam-sākhīs on the other is the janaṁ-sākhīs' deep involvement in the issue of reconciliation between Hindu and Muslim, a theme which runs right through the literature from the united welcome accorded the baby Nānak at his birth to the final dispute concerning the proper disposal of his body. It is strongly implied in the terminology used to designate the Gurū and it is explicitly stated at several points in all janam-sākhī traditions.

The janam-sākhī attitude towards this issue must be clearly distinguished from Gurū Nānak's own attitude. The latter can be easily ascertained from the Gurū's works recorded in the *Ādi Granth* where we find a conviction which interprets reconciliation in terms of an ultimate transcending of both Hindu and Muslim beliefs. The attitude to which the janam-sākhīs bear witness is the attitude of the Sikh Panth at a remove of some seventy or a hundred years from the Gurū's death. Although it cannot be said that the understanding which we find expressed therein is positively opposed to that of Gurū Nānak, it is not possible to affirm a total accord. The janam-sākhī understanding is pitched at a somewhat lower level, one which represents the Gurū as a Hindu to Hindus and a Muslim to Muslims, as one who 'dressed as a *bairāgī* and as a *faqīr*'. An indignant administrator regards him as a Hindu and Bābā Nānak is himself made to say, 'I am a Hindu.' This information he communicates to some faqīrs while journeying to Mecca and the faqīrs report it when they reach the city a year later. The people of Mecca have, however, formed a different opinion. 'This is no Hindu!' they declared. 'This is a great sage, one who recites the *namāz*. Everyone recites the *namāz* after him. He recites the *namāz* before anyone else.' 'He told us, "I am a Hindu",' explained the faqīrs, 'but in reality he is a Muslim and thus he has come near to God.'[6]

This narrative obviously represented a dominant conviction amongst Gurū Nānak's later followers and one which in the early seventeenth century must have commanded a considerable attention. It is an issue which illustrates the link between the historical Nānak and the testimony of the janam-sākhīs; and which at the same time plainly indicates how that testimony has moved away from the historical Nānak. The issue leads us from our second to our third point. We are now moving within the janam-sākhīs' own period, examining not the life and teachings of Gurū Nānak, but a later interpretation of that life and those teachings. It is essential that this distinction should be understood.

The early janam-sākhīs evolved during the period which extends from the late sixteenth century throughout the seventeenth century. This was unquestionably their season of major development and we must bear in mind that it precedes an unusually significant period in Pañjāb history. It precedes that tumultuous century which stretches from the founding of the Khālsā in A.D. 1699 through to the emergence of Mahārājā Rañjīt Siṅgh. The early janam-sākhīs evolved during the pre-Khālsā period and this fact serves to underline their importance as sources of Pañjāb history. Our understanding of pre-Khālsā history has been moulded in large measure by post-Khālsā assumptions, and a source which lacks these assumptions acquires thereby an added significance.

The society within which the janam-sākhīs evolved was, of course, the emergent Panth and to this we can add that it was clearly a rural society. The imagery is rural, the various characters normally follow rural pursuits, and on the rare occasions when the Gurū is taken by the authors into a city there is little

[6] *B40* janam-sākhī (India Office Library MS. Panj. B40), f. 129a.

awareness of the nature of urban life. The only exception to this, and that a very partial one, is the relatively sophisticated Miharbān who had evidently paid some visits to Lahore. This rural base will occasion no surprise and we do not need the janam-sākhīs to tell us that Pañjāb society was overwhelmingly rural during this period. In order to appreciate the janam-sākhīs we must, however, retain an awareness of this background. The locus of the janam-sākhīs is rural Pañjāb and it is a rural understanding which finds expression in them. We must also observe that it is an understanding conditioned and in large measure dominated by an amalgam of Puranic and Nāth legend. The janam-sākhīs bear overwhelming witness to this feature.

As one would expect, the fact that the janam-sākhīs evolved within a rising religious society has left a dominant impress upon the material which they offer. Religious issues are the primary concern of the authors and predictably we are treated to lengthy discourses on the way of salvation. Let it not be assumed, however, that these discourses offer nothing that will satisfy a wider historical interest. Religion was not, for the authors of the janam-sākhīs or their audiences, a set of doctrines. It extended far beyond this, ramifying throughout their society.

Inevitably the janam-sākhī narrators make repeated references to this society, few of them deliberate or contrived. We observe, in the first place, a developing self-consciousness, a growing awareness of the nature and function of the Panth as a distinctive religious group. It is by no means as coherent as it was to become in the eighteenth century, but the development is clearly taking place. In the janam-sākhīs it is possible to perceive a consciousness of distinction within the wider Pañjāb society.

Go, Nānak, [answered God]. Your Panth will flourish. The salutation of your followers shall be: 'In the name of the True Gurū I fall at your feet'. The salutation of the Vaiṣṇava Panth is: 'In the name of Rāma and Kriṣṇa'. The salutation of the Sanyāsī Panth is: 'In the name of Nārāyaṇ I bow before you'. The yogīs' salutation is: 'Hail to the Primal One'. The Muslims' cry is: 'In the name of the One God peace be with you'. You are Nānak and your Panth will flourish. Your followers shall be called Nānak-panthīs and their salutation shall be: 'In the name of the True Gurū I fall at your feet'. I shall bless your Panth. Inculcate devotion towards Me and strengthen men's obedience to their *dharma*. As the Vaiṣṇavas have their temple, the yogīs their *āsaṇ*, and the Muslims their mosque, so your followers shall have their dharamsālā. Three things you must inculcate in your Panth: repeating the divine Name, giving charity, and regular bathing. Keep yourself unspotted while yet remaining a householder.[7]

The awareness of difference is plainly evident, but it is not a difference which implies total separation. We must bear in mind the eirenic insistence of the janam-sākhīs upon the need for an understanding between Hindus and Muslims. The distinctiveness of the Panth is obviously assumed, but it is a distinctiveness set within a wider unity.

From the repeated references to the erection and use of dharamsālās it is clear that these buildings stood at the centre of the corporate life of the Panth and that much activity must have been conducted within them. When the hostile administrator is converted the first thing he does after donating land is to erect a dharamsālā and the *Miharbān Janam-sākhī* sets numerous discourses within the walls of this particular structure. The *B40* janam-sākhī concludes many of its individual stories with the statement that 'a dharamsālā was built' and the *Hāfizābād Janam-sākhī*, concluding its account of how a *ṭhag* named Sajjan was converted, makes pointed reference to the erection of 'the first dharamsālā'. These buildings obviously corresponded to the modern gurdwara, not to the hospice variety of dharamsālā which serves the needs of travellers and visitors. No indication is given of substantial size or ornamentation and we may accordingly assume that they were invariably simple structures, or single rooms set aside for this devotional purpose.

A particularly vivid picture of a saṅgat at worship in a dharamsālā is given in the *B40* janam-sākhī's account of how a childless rājā was granted a son by Bābā Nānak.

Beneath the rājā's palace was the dharamsālā where the Sikhs sang hymns and performed *kīrtan*. Sitting there the rājā would fix his attention on the music of whatever hymn the Sikhs were singing. One day the rānī said to the rājā, 'Rājā, how is it that no children have been born in our house? Let us go to the dharamsālā and lay our petition before the congregation, for the Gurū is present in the congregation.' 'An excellent idea!' replied the rājā.

[7] Ibid., f. 120b.

Next day the rājā and the rānī both joined the congregation. It was an *Ekādasī* gathering. There was a congregational festival (*melā*) and a large congregation was present. A hymn was being sung and all were sitting enthralled. The rājā and the rānī then presented their petition, saying, 'You are the assembly of the Gurū and whatever is sought from you is granted. May it please you to hear our intercession so that the Gurū may grant a son.'

Those who were present in the congregation offered a prayer in order that the rājā's faith might remain unshaken. Then they assured him, 'The Gurū Bābā will grant you a son.'[8]

This not only provides a glimpse of a seventeenth-century Sikh congregation, but also indicates an early phase in the development of the doctrine of the *Gurū Panth*.[9]

Reference is made both in the passage just quoted and in many other places to the centrality of congregational singing (*kīrtan*) in the life of the Panth and from some references it is clear that certain selections of scripture had already acquired a liturgical function. For the compiler of the *B40* janam-sākhī the important liturgical office was evidently the selection of hymns called the *Āratī Sohilā* which is traditionally sung or recited before gong to bed. 'When Bābā Nānak was no longer listening the musician (*rabābī*) would sing the *Āratī Sohilā*. When he had sung the *Āratī Sohilā* there would come the command: "Go aside, my Sikhs, and sleep." The Sikhs would then go to sleep.'[10]

No reference is made in this janam-sākhī to the other traditional evening office, the *Sodar Rahirās*. A reference in another janam-sākhī indicates that it must have evolved by the early seventeenth century, but the silence of the *B40* janam-sākhī suggests that the practice was not followed universally during that century.

At certain points, particularly in the discourse material, a writer will introduce a question which must have been asked within the Sikh saṅgats, and then either give a direct answer or else narrate a symbolic response. ' "Nānak," asked Sheikh Ibrāhīm, "tell me, does grace follow service, does service follow grace?" '[11] To this question Bābā Nānak replies: 'First is his service, Sheikhjī, and if anyone perform it humbly God will

[8] Ibid., ff. 191b–192a.
[9] See below, pp. 45–50.
[10] *B40* janam-sākhī, f. 97b.
[11] Ibid., f. 56b.

bestow the virtue of piety upon him. If, however, a man performs service but is puffed up with pride, then even though his service be of a high order the Lord will not come near him. He will be rejected. The price [of grace], Sheikhjī, is service.'[12] For the Gurū Nānak of the *Ādi Granth* divine grace and human endeavour run parallel, both being vital to salvation. The only hint of priority comes in the indication that man's initial perception of the way of salvation is the result of grace. For the janam-sākhī writers, however, it is the other way round. Grace must be earned.

Many other doctrinal questions appear during the course of the narratives. A peasant in a place called 'the Land of Unbelievers' asks, 'Without having seen Him how can one know there is a God?' To this the janam-sākhī writers have no satisfactory direct answer and so resort to a miracle to make the point. Mardānā, a frequent companion of the Gurū, asks after having witnessed Bābur's destruction of the town of Saidpur, 'Why have so many been slain when only one did wrong?' In some cases brief answers are supplied to such questions; in others (as we have just noted) a convenient miracle resolves the difficulty; and in yet others we are given lengthy doctrinal statements which do much to illuminate beliefs which were evidently held within the Panth during the seventeenth century. No point receives greater emphasis than the repeated insistence upon the absolute efficacy of the divine Name. ' "Previously men performed austerities for a hundred thousand years," said Bābā Nānak to Kaliyug, "but in your age if anyone meditates upon the divine Name with undivided attention for a single *gharī* he will be saved." '[13] This is a strikingly different emphasis from that which we find in the eighteenth-century Khālsā traditions.

Beyond the narrower bounds of doctrine and the practice of meditation we can observe certain social responses which flow from the religious convictions of the Panth. One which we would expect and which we do indeed find is a strong opposition to notions of caste or ritual purity. The scorn which is cast upon the ritually punctilious reflects not merely the teaching of Gurū Nānak but also the positive acceptance of this particular teaching by his later followers.

[12] Ibid., f. 57a.

[13] Ibid., f. 42a.

Another prominent feature, one which departs in some measure from the teachings of the Gurū, is a marked deference to the ascetic ideal. At certain points we encounter statements directed against the futility of austerities, statements which are in total accord with the words of Gurū Nānak. There is, for example, the answer which the Sikh trader Mansukh is said to have given to the King of Srī Laṅkā: 'I have already obtained the thing for which you perform fasts, religious observances, and discipline. Why then should I fast and perform these religious observances?'[14] The dominant emphasis is, however, opposed to this. Gurū Nānak himself is made to say: 'I have met so many people of this world. Let me leave them and dwell apart. Here there is the tumult of great numbers. What is there for me to obtain in the world? I shall go apart from the world, in seclusion and in hiding, and remaining there I shall meditate on God.'[15] Elsewhere the merit of austerities is vigorously affirmed and renunciants, both Hindu and Muslim, are treated with considerable respect.

We also find in the janam-sākhīs' choice of subject and treatment indications of some controversies which evidently troubled the Panth and which in certain cases extend beyond the area of doctrine to that of social behaviour. The most prominent of all relates to the question of whether or not the early-morning bathe should be obligatory, and from the amount of space devoted to the question we can only conclude that it must have been an issue of some concern. It is the *Miharbān* tradition which devotes the most attention to the question. The narrator's own mind is quite made up—the early-morning bathe is absolutely essential—but he has a problem. The *Miharbān* method is always to quote an extract from the works of Gurū Nānak in order to prove his point, but in this particular case no such extract can be found. First the narrator quotes a passage which has no possible bearing on the subject. Next he uses one which does indeed refer to bathing, but unfortunately contradicts his own point as it plainly says that the only essential bathing is a spiritual bathing in the divine Word. Finally he solves the problem by quoting an appropriate passage from the works of Gurū Aṅgad, putting it instead into the mouth of Gurū Nānak.[16]

[14] Ibid., f. 137b. [15] Ibid., f. 101b.

[16] *Janam-Sākhī Srī Gurū Nānak Dev Jī, likhat Srī Miharbān Jī Soḍhī*, Vol. 2 (Amritsar, 1969), p. xi.

Another issue has evidently been the question of whether or not the followers of Gurū Nānak might eat meat, although this one appears to have emerged somewhat later. Early janam-sākhīs indicate that it was definitely permitted, and it is only in later nineteenth-century versions that the question is seriously raised.[17] We may also note in passing that an incident recorded in the *B40* janam-sākhī indicates that at least some early Sikhs had no problems about cutting hair. A poor Sikh, unable to provide food for the Gurū, sells his hair and fulfils the requirements of hospitality with the proceeds. For this deed he is warmly commended by the Gurū.[18] Earlier we referred to the fact that the janam-sākhīs reflect pre-Khālsā Sikh society. To this we can add the claim that at certain points they reflect a condition prior to the firm establishment of Jaṭ patterns. No story illustrates the fact more dramatically than this hair-cutting episode.[19]

Comments of this kind concern the more obvious issues. They warrant a particular interest, but in bestowing this we must not overlook the host of passing references which together constitute a fascinating picture of the rural Pañjāb within which the janam-sākhī authors lived. Even when a narrative purports to represent some distant country its detailed descriptions will normally relate to the known Pañjāb of the writer's experience rather than to the unknown foreign place. These details are inconspicuous simply because they are so ordinary, and they should not for this reason be treated as insignificant. Needless to say, it is not possible to write a social or economic history of seventeenth-century Pañjāb from the janam-sākhīs alone, but they do nevertheless provide many useful glimpses of the period.

A catalogue of these passing references could run to great length. We are given glimpses of birth ceremonies, naming ceremonies, marriages, and funerals. A child sits with his teacher and is shown how to read. Labourers bring in the harvest for threshing or carry grass to the village for the buffaloes. Women attend to their cooking duties in their well-plastered kitchens. A Vaiṣṇava holy man appears, complete with tulsī-garland, sacred stone, rosary, and frontal mark. Sūfī pīrs pass in litters

[17] W. H. McLeod, op. cit., p. 84n.

[18] *B40* janam-sākhī, f. 44a.

[19] The impact of Jaṭ customs is discussed in the third essay. See below, pp. 50–51.

and descend to greet their equals with the approved salutation. Nāth yogīs, squatting beside their hearths, pass round their intoxicating brew of molasses and *mahūā* petals. Many Muslims are to be seen in regular attendance at the mosque, but others less faithful neglect their prayers and instead devote their attention to the consumption of hashish and liquor. A scrupulous brāhmaṇ carefully prepares his ritually pure cooking-square. A band of pilgrims pass by on their way to a celebrated shrine.

Most prominent of all is the one who tramps the dusty roads or sits upon his string-bed under the shade of a pīpal tree, the man who with his ninth and last successor occupies a position of unrivalled affection and influence in the corporate memory of the Pañjāb. It may not be an entirely accurate representation of the actual man who was born five hundred years ago, but certainly it is a faithful representation of an image which exercised an immense influence on his seventeenth-century followers. This is the Gurū Nānak to whom the janam-sākhīs bear witness, and herein too lies a considerable measure of their value. It is an image which testifies to the fact that in history what is believed to have happened can commonly be more important than what actually did happen.

3

COHESIVE IDEALS AND INSTITUTIONS IN THE HISTORY OF THE SIKH PANTH

WHO is a Sikh and how is the Sikh Panth to be defined? At one level the answer is easily given. A Sikh is one who believes in the religion of the ten Gurūs and in no other. The primary criterion is strictly religious and it is accordingly on the basis of a distinctive religious belief and practice that the Panth's identity is to be established.

There are, however, serious problems to be encountered when this investigation is pressed further. The diverse constituency of the Panth has already been noted, with a particular emphasis laid upon the numerical dominance of Jaṭs. Although religious belief can provide a powerful bond it would nevertheless be naïve to assume that the conventional values of Jaṭs, Khatrīs, and others would involve no tensions within a religious grouping which included such distinctively different groups. There are, moreover, the conflicts which can arise from the characteristically powerful adherence of Jaṭs to narrower family and factional loyalties.[1] Inevitably these tensions are reflected in Sikh history and in the specifics developed for the maintenance of the evolving Panth's cohesion. Throughout Sikh history we observe a theory of religious unity contending with a diversity of social elements. This we find set within a context where lines of distinction are easily blurred. Periods of particular difficulty have been experienced during the waning of the original religious impulse, the persecution of the early eighteenth century, the anarchy of the mid- and later eighteenth century, the confused years which followed the death of Mahārājā Rañjīt Singh in 1839, and the twentieth-century diaspora. All of these have raised acute problems of identity and cohesion, and have with varying success produced distinctive solutions.

[1] For an important analysis of contemporary factionalism within the Jaṭ community see Joyce Pettigrew, *Robber Noblemen: A Study of the Political System of the Sikh Jats* (London, 1975).

There is a sound practical reason why a functional analysis of this kind is so important in the area of Sikh studies. The analysis is necessary because the Panth is currently passing through another of its periodic identity crises and because the crisis now constitutes a significant aspect of a particular immigrant situation. Within the Pañjāb itself many of the younger Sikhs are disregarding their traditional symbols and discipline with increasing boldness. In some instances the rebellion amounts to no more than a covert trimming of the beard; in others it is an open rejection which extends to the use of that unlawful substance tobacco. Amongst the migrant Sikhs living in the United Kingdom this trend has been even more pronounced. The extent to which the old discipline has been abandoned can be appreciated only when we remind ourselves that at least three-quarters of the Indian immigrants in the United Kingdom are Sikhs.[2] This statement commonly evokes an incredulous response, for it is obvious that a majority of these immigrants no longer look like Sikhs. And this is precisely the problem as the orthodox Sikhs see it. More and more of their brethren are earning for themselves the title of *patit*, or 'apostate', by removing their turbans and cutting their hair.

It is generally assumed that Sikh history begins with Gurū Nānak. For present purposes this assumption can be accepted. Although many relevant developments predate this period,[3] such antecedents need not deflect the analysis at this point. The analysis concerns the Sikh Panth and there can be no doubt that the Panth originated in the loose following which gathered around Bābā Nānak during the first four decades of the sixteenth century.

In this earliest phase no specific agent was needed to maintain the cohesion of the Panth. All that was required was provided by the direct personal loyalty of the disciple who had voluntarily elected to place himself under this particular Master. The Master was present in the flesh and his word would certainly have been accepted as law by his more devout followers. Countless religious panths of this informal kind have risen in India and then slowly disappeared. This particular panth not

[2] E. J. B. Rose, *Colour and Citizenship* (London, 1969), p. 52. Roger T. Bell, writing in *New Backgrounds: the Immigrant Child at Home and at School*, ed. Robin Oakley (London, 1968), p. 52, gives the proportion as 80 per cent.

[3] See above, pp. 5–7.

only survived but also expanded, and inevitably it experienced in the process a need for something more than the personality of the first Master.

The personality of the first Master has, however, been of continuing importance as a cohesive factor, one which still survives to this day. Nānak's own personal influence in terms of Sikh cohesion was extended beyond his death in two distinct ways. The first protraction consisted of the line of successors who followed him as Gurūs of the community. The succession did not always take place without a dispute (Sikh history has also had its anti-popes), but in spite of these occasional difficulties the line continued unbroken up to the death of the tenth Gurū, Gobind Siṅgh, in 1708. Sikh tradition makes it abundantly clear that this line of Gurūs is not to be understood as a succession of one person following another. It is interpreted as one person following himself. There were ten Nānaks or, more precisely, ten manifestations in different bodies of the one original Nānak commissioned by God and sent into the world for the salvation of mankind.

The figure which is most commonly employed to express this doctrine is the conventional image of a torch lit from another torch. The actual torches may be different, but the flame is the same. The bodies may be different, but they are inhabited by the same spirit. Elsewhere the image is varied. Lahaṇā, the second Gurū, is renamed Aṅgad because he was an *aṅg*, or 'limb', from Nānak's own body. Nānak's formal investiture of Aṅgad as his successor is represented as light blending with light, and the divine origin of this light is stressed when the same idiom is used to describe Nānak's death. The *Ādi Granth* contains the works of six of the Gurūs, but these six own only one name. All are called Nānak.

There can be no doubt that the function of this doctrine was a simple extension of the first Gurū's authority and in this manner it continued to serve a cohesive role for more than a century and a half. It was not entirely successful, for some of the disappointed contenders to the succession did manage to attach followings of indeterminate size to their particular versions of the light. There was, however, no question about the majority allegiance and until the death of Gobind Siṅgh the office of Gurū served the cohesive role with a notable distinction. The crisis came at the death of the tenth Gurū because Gobind Siṅgh's sons had all predeceased him. During the late sixteenth century the office had become hereditary in the family of Soḍhī Khatrīs descended from the fourth Gurū, Rām Dās, himself the son-in-law of the third Gurū. Although this custom greatly restricted the number of possible claimants, it created serious dislocation when the tenth Gurū died without heirs. We shall see later how the dilemma was eventually resolved.

The second means of protracting the personal authority of the first Gurū was provided by the janam-sākhīs, the hagiographic accounts of Nānak which were described in the second essay. In the case of the janam-sākhīs function must be distinguished from purpose. The various compilers make their purpose clear by means of comments sprinkled throughout their collections of anecdotes, and commonly reinforce it with a concluding declaration. Their express purpose is soteriological.

> He who reads or hears this [janam-] sākhī shall attain to the supreme rapture. He who hears, sings, or reads this [janam-] sākhī shall find his highest desire fulfilled, for through it he shall meet Gurū Bābā [Nānak, the giver of salvation]. He who with love sings of the glory of Bābā [Nānak] or gives ear to it shall obtain joy ineffable in all that he does in this life, and in the life to come salvation.[4]

The intention, plainly, is to confirm and strengthen the believer, and to attract others to the same belief. In so far as they succeeded, the janam-sākhīs fulfilled (and continue to fulfil) the purpose for which they were recorded and circulated.

The latent function of the janam-sākhīs is, however, rather different. It is as a cohesive agent that the janam-sākhī literature has been of particular importance in the Panth, especially during its pre-Khālsā period. Whereas the purpose of the janam-sākhīs concerned the individual, their function has concerned the community as a whole. By persistently directing attention to the person of the first Gurū the janam-sākhīs provided a single focus, a common loyalty to which all members of the Panth could adhere. This personality received far more attention than any distinctive doctrine, and although the later janam-sākhī narrators are by no means uninterested in doctrinal issues

[4] Piar Singh (ed.), *Sambhū Nāth vālī Janam-patrī Bābe Nānak Jī kī prasidh nān Ādi Sākhīān* (Patiala, 1969), p. 101.

they invariably relate such issues directly to their image of Bābā Nānak. Anything which concerns belief or practice is incorporated in the narrative and is there represented as a statement uttered by Nānak or as an action performed by him. Janam-sākhīs of later Gurūs are conspicuous by their absence. Everything clusters around a single centre. If a person owes and owns allegiance to this single centre he is a *Nānak-panthī*, a Sikh of Gurū Nānak.

This cohesive role the janam-sākhīs performed with notable success for more than a century. It was as the constituency of the Panth became increasingly dominated by the growing Jaṭ membership that their effectiveness began to dwindle. There is evidence which suggests that one of the major traditions, the *Bālā* tradition, represents a distinctively Jaṭ venture into the field of janam-sākhī composition, and that here as in other respects the first response to their increasing dominance was a simple recasting of existing institutions. This particular institution related, however, to a pattern which was being superseded. The distinctively religious emphasis of the earlier Panth was losing its force. Its ideals were being replaced by concepts which derived from the culture of the Jaṭs. The more restricted religious interpretation survived, but increasingly it was pushed away to the periphery of Sikh life. Its recession was matched by a decline in the effectiveness of the janam-sākhī. It would not, of course, be true to suggest that they had become positively dysfunctional. Only in these days of wider education and growing scepticism is this situation developing. They were, nevertheless, losing much of their efficacy and in the confusion which followed the death of Gurū Gobind Siṅgh the need for functional subtsitutes became acute.

Before reviewing the new pattern which emerged from this period of confusion it will be convenient to return to the earliest years of the Panth and briefly to trace the developments which finally issued in the eighteenth-century crisis. In the first essay it was suggested that although the pattern established by Gurū Nānak must have continued with little change under his first successor, supplementary features do become evident during the period of the third Gurū, Amar Dās.[5] By this time the bonds of personal commitment were apparently proving in-

[5] See above, pp. 7–10.

sufficient for the maintenance of the Panth's pristine cohesion. To this end Gurū Amar Dās encouraged his disciples to regard Goindvāl, where he resided, as a place of pilgrimage. Three of the traditional Hindu festivals became the occasions of large gatherings in Goindvāl, and tradition also accords to Gurū Amar Dās a decision to institute distinctively Sikh ceremonies for birth, marriage, and death.

All of these customs have served a cohesive function and even if tradition errs in ascribing them to the third Gurū there can be no doubt that they must have developed at a relatively early date. The same concern for the cohesion of the Panth must also have been responsible for the practice of appointing leaders of local congregations, commissioned by the Gurū to exercise certain aspects of his authority in areas away from Goindvāl. Although the actual details are exceedingly obscure it is evident that Gurū Amar Dās organized a system of *mañjīs* (literally 'string-bed' but meaning 'seat of authority') and that the individual appointed to a *mañjī* came to be called a *masand*. Under the fourth Gurū the actual centre of this growing network was moved a short distance away from Goindvāl to the new village of Rāmdāspur. This subsequently acquired the name Amritsar and although during the later seventeenth century its status was overshadowed by Śivālik sites it recovered during the early eighteenth century and has remained the unchallenged centre ever since.

These developments during the period of the third and fourth Gurūs supplemented the role of the personal Gurū and that of the janam-sākhīs. Had the Panth preserved its original pattern the combination would doubtless have been adequate for at least two hundred years and probably for even longer. The Panth would have lived in relative peace, it would probably have remained restricted in size, and it would certainly have lacked clarity of definition. The pattern did not, however, continue unchanged. It was transformed, as we have already seen, by the adherence of increasing numbers of Jaṭs. This produced not only new problems of cohesion, but also distinctive solutions. These solutions were in turn modified by the entry of Aroṛās, particularly during the early nineteenth century, and later still by the numerous outcastes who accepted the Khālsā discipline around the turn of the century.

At what point in time did these problems first become manifest? This is very difficult to answer. It is possible that one of the early succession disputes reflects the changing constitution of the Panth and that the truly radical changes were considerably delayed because victory went to the side which best accorded with Jaṭ expectations. This was the dispute which followed the death of the fourth Gurū, Rām Dās, in 1581. Gurū Rām Dās was succeeded not by his eldest son, Prithī Chand, but by his youngest son, Arjan. That at least is how the succession is represented in later tradition. In actual fact there was a division of the Panth between the followers of Prithī Chand and those of Arjan, with both leaders assuming the title of Gurū. It is now very difficult to envisage this situation, for our impressions have been deeply dyed in subsequent polemic. Although much invective must have issued from both sides we now possess little except that of the victors. This represents the followers of Prithī Chand as dissembling scoundrels and the name applied to them (Mīṇās) means precisely that. They are one of the five execrated groups which Khālsā Sikhs must, at the time of baptism, promise to spurn, and although the sect is now extinct its unhappy reputation lives on. The fact that the *Miharbān Janam-sākhī* was produced by this group means that a deep distrust still attaches to that janam-sākhī.[6]

It is accordingly assumed without any question that the segment of the Panth which elected to follow Prithī Chand represented a malignant heresy. A study of the *Miharbān Janam-sākhī* leads us to reject this traditional interpretation. Whatever else the Mīṇās may have been they certainly were not heretics, at least not if their surviving literature is any guide. Their literature suggests that this particular group may have been seeking to restrict the Panth's concerns to the more limited religious aspects of Nānak's teachings, that they were opposed to the wider social concern which increasingly occupied the Panth's interest and which increasingly was being used to define its nature.

Interesting though this speculation may be we must refrain from pressing it any further, for it is still little more than speculation. All we are entitled to affirm at this stage is that during the early years of the seventeenth century the pattern of Sikh

[6] See above, p. 24.

behaviour underwent a change which carried it some distance away from the religious concerns of Nānak and closer to the characteristic pattern of Jaṭ culture. It is, at this point in time, still only a tendency and although it was obviously a strong one it had not yet issued in a radical break with the past. Khatrī leadership continued and during the time of the seventh Gurū there was actually a movement back towards the earlier pattern. The personal Gurū was still the principal agent of cohesion and still a generally effective one. The truly radical break comes with the death of the tenth Gurū. This raised the question of authority (and so of the Panth's cohesion) in an exceedingly acute form. To whom should the Sikh's allegiance now be due? Who (or what) could now hold the Panth together?

Reference has already been made to the traditional version of how authority within the Panth was transferred at the time of Gurū Gobind Siṅgh's death. According to tradition, the question of authority was determined by a clear pronouncement uttered by Gurū Gobind Siṅgh at the point of death. The line of personal Gurūs was to come to an end and the functions of the Gurū were to vest jointly in the scripture and in the Panth. It seems clear that, as in so many other cases, the single event recorded in tradition must be replaced by an extended period of evolution. Well before the death of Gurū Gobind Siṅgh we can perceive in the literature of the earlier seventeenth century indications of a developing doctrine of the *Gurū Panth*, a doctrine which affirms that in the absence of the personal Gurū the local saṅgat, or congregation, within any area possesses the mystical power to make decisions on his behalf.[7]

The death of Gurū Gobind Siṅgh did indeed mark a crucial stage in this development, but not necessarily one which depended upon a personal pronouncement. We have already noted how, from the time of the fourth Gurū onwards, the office of Gurū remained hereditary within the Soḍhī family. Gurū Gobind Siṅgh had sons, but all had predeceased him and when he died in 1708 he was without an heir. This situation resulted in a leadership vacuum which was solved only in the course of time. The first answer appears to have been the personal leadership of Bandā. It was, however, a failure and even during his lifetime

[7] Another convention which had appeared prior to the time of Gurū Gobind Siṅgh was the use of the term *khālsā* to designate the Panth. J. S. Grewal and S. S. Bal, *Guru Gobind Singh* (Chandigarh, 1967), p. 115.

it was evidently a disputed answer. Following his death the Sikhs were scattered and a new theory of leadership was needed. The same problem persisted throughout the period of the misls. A pattern was required which would permit ample freedom to the small group while at the same time preserving a theory of unified authority, and it was essential that this theory should possess a powerful sanction. During the latter half of the eighteenth century latent enmities produced a series of shifting alliances and open conflicts between individual misls. The factional disputes which command such importance in Jaṭ society today evidently had their parallels in the misls of the eighteenth century.[8]

An answer to the need was provided by the doctrine of the corporate and scriptural Gurū. During the eighteenth century it was the corporate aspect of the doctrine which possessed the greater importance and which served to impart a measure of cohesion to the community. Later, as we shall see, the doctrine of the corporate Gurū effectively lapsed and an undisputed primacy was assumed by the scriptural Gurū theory, a primacy which continues to this day.

It would perhaps be wise to summarize at this point the eighteenth-century political and military developments which were covered in the first essay. Bandā's execution in 1716 was followed by a period of more than a decade during which the Mughal authorities attempted to bring the increasingly turbulent Jaṭ Sikhs under control. The Sikhs retaliated by organizing themselves into numerous small and highly mobile bands called *jathās*, each commanded by a *jathedār*. Recognizing the need for some sort of unified strategy the jathedārs evidently attempted to devise a confederation by meeting on the occasion of the Baisākhī and Dīvālī festivals. Although these meetings cannot have been held regularly they nevertheless expressed a continuing concern for solidarity and for some sort of common authority. At these gatherings the jathās were regarded as constituting the *Sarbat Khālsā*, or 'Entire Khālsā'. When during the fourth decade of the century efforts were made to extend the joint meetings to joint campaigning the resultant army (which generally existed in theory rather than in fact) was called the *Dal Khālsā*, the 'Khālsā Army'.

[8] Joyce Pettigrew, op. cit., esp. chap. 3, 'Significant Events in Jat History'.

Until the middle of the century these attempts to forge a permanent union of the jathās were conspicuously unsuccessful, particularly when the declining Mughal administration relaxed its efforts to control them. A closer unity did not develop until Ahmad Shāh Abdālī began his series of invasions from Afghanistan. The first of these was launched in 1747 and the last finally petered out in 1769. Ahmad Shāh Abdālī succeeded in defeating both the Mughals and the Marāṭhās, but he did not succeed in quelling the Sikhs. On the contrary, they grew and flourished, stimulated by the challenge of an external invasion. The invader in this particular instance added a religious dimension to the conflict, with the result that the distinctively Sikh character of the resistance was considerably strengthened. Ahmad Shāh Abdālī did much to restore unity to the Sikh ranks and at the same time to strengthen their self-awareness as Sikhs and their opposition to Muslims.

Even this, however, was not sufficient to develop a durable unity. Shortly after the beginning of the Afghān invasions the numerous small jathās had regrouped as twelve larger bands. These were the twelve misls, each commanding an ill-defined territory and each led by its own *sardār*, or chieftain. These misls were essentially independent, but the pressure of the Afghān invasions had been sufficient to compress them into a reasonably compact group, dominated by Jassā Siṅgh of the Āhlūwālīā misl. When the Afghān threat was removed the misls quickly drifted apart and soon fell to internecine warfare. Eventually the Śukerchakiā misl threw up in Rañjīt Siṅgh a leader of unusual ability and the ascendancy of this misl finally achieved by military means the unity which the Sikhs had sought for so long.[9]

A characteristic feature of the century which led up to this climax was, for the Sikhs, dispersion. The jathās were widely scattered and so too were the continuing congregations (*saṅgats*). Within both jathā and saṅgat the instrument of authority increasingly came to be identified with the group itself. The Gurū was present in the saṅgat and the corporate voice of the saṅgat was accordingly the voice of the Gurū. The saṅgat provided a

[9] For Ahmad Shāh Abdālī and the rise of the Sikh misls see Ganda Singh, *Ahmad Shah Durrani* (Bombay, 1959); Narendra Krishna Sinha, *Rise of the Sikh Power* (Calcutta, 2nd ed., 1946); H. R. Gupta, *History of the Sikhs*, Vol. 1 (Calcutta, 1939), Vols. 2 and 3 (Lahore, 1944).

religious context and the jathā a military extension of the same idea.

The termination of the line of personal Gurūs and the failure of Bandā to continue it had thus produced a new pattern. During the period of the personal Gurūs the problems encountered by the more distant saṅgats had already prompted the idea of the Gurū's presence within the local congregation. With the permanent removal of the Gurū's physical presence this doctrine was magnified in importance and during the middle years of the eighteenth century it assumed a position of primacy within the Panth. The Gurū, though absent in the body, is very much present in spirit wherever his words are devoutly sung. They who with genuine devotion participate in this *kīrtan* (communal singing) manifest in their assembly the Gurū's own presence, and when they speak as an assembly they speak as the Gurū. If for any particular purpose a limited number of participants was required, five representatives (the *pañj piāre* or 'five beloved') were chosen and temporarily invested with the authority of the saṅgat.

For its kīrtan sessions and other religious assemblies each saṅgat set aside a particular room or building. This was the *dharamsālā*, or prototype gurdwara, an institution which was briefly described earlier.[10] The frequency with which the dharamsālā is mentioned in the janam-sākhīs indicates that for the Sikhs of the seventeenth and early eighteenth centuries it occupied a central position in the life of the community. This role was substantially weakened later in the eighteenth century as the Khālsā rose to prominence. The energies of the Khālsā were largely absorbed in activities other than the devotional concerns of the dharamsālā and although some of the principal sites retained a considerable reverence many of the minor ones were allowed to remain the preserve of non-Khālsā Sikhs.

In this manner military needs and the extension of Khālsā influence shifted the Panth's primary interests away from the saṅgat towards the jathā and later the misl. This shift of interest carried with it the same belief in a mystical presence of the Gurū. As military and eventually political issues began to command an increasing attention, the doctrine was extended to cover the quasi-parliamentary sessions of the Sarbat Khālsā.

[10] See above, p. 31.

The need for cohesion did not end at the local saṅgat. The misl sardārs also had their problems to solve and the doctrine of the *Gurū Panth* proved to be well suited to their needs.

This doctrine eventually found an explicit practical expression in the institution of the gurmattā, in the theory that corporate decisions of the Sarbat Khālsā were to be regarded as the word of the Gurū with the full force of his authority to back it. The gurmattā is an unusually interesting feature of Sikh history, one which in any account of the period warrants more than a passing reference. During the invasions of Ahmad Shāh Abdālī it provided a useful means of deciding joint action, and it seems safe to assume that the disunity of the misl period would have been much more serious but for the respect accorded this institution.

The word *gurmattā* is a compound term meaning, literally, 'the mind, or intention, of the Gurū'. It was not, as some writers have assumed, a meeting of the Sarbat Khālsā, but rather a resolution passed at such a meeting. Sir John Malcolm was evidently responsible for this confusion. His description of the procedure is, however, worth quoting, for it is based upon inquiries made in 1805 and is accordingly one of the earliest accounts available.

When a Gúrú-matá, or great national council, is called, as it always is, or ought to be, when any imminent danger threatens the country, or any large expedition is to be undertaken, all the Sikh chiefs assemble at Amritsar. The assembly, which is called the Gúrú-matá, is convened by the Acális; and when the chiefs meet upon this solemn occasion, it is concluded that all private animosities cease and that every man sacrifices his personal feelings at the shrine of the general good; and, actuated by principles of pure patriotism, thinks of nothing but the interests of the religion and commonwealth to which he belongs.

When the chiefs and principal leaders are seated, the Adi-Grant'h and Daśama Pádsháh ka Grant'h are placed before them. They all bend their heads before these scriptures, and exclaim, *Wa! Gúrúji ka Khálsa! Wa! Gúrúji ki Fateh!* A great quantity of cakes made of wheat, butter, and sugar, are then placed before the volumes of the sacred writings, and covered with a cloth. These holy cakes, which are in commemoration of the injunction of Nánac, to eat and to give to others to eat, next receive the salutations of the assembly, who then rise and the Acális pray aloud, while the musicians play. The Acális, when the prayers are finished, desire the council to be seated. They sit down, and the cakes being uncovered, are eaten of by all classes of Sikhs: those distinctions of original tribes, which are, on other occasions kept up, being on this occasion laid aside, in token of their general and complete union in one cause. The Acális then exclaim: 'Sirdars! (chiefs) this is a Gúrú-matá!' on which prayers are again said aloud. The chiefs, after this, sit closer and say to each other: 'The sacred Grant'h is betwixt us, let us swear by our scripture to forget all internal disputes and to be united.' This moment of religious fervor and ardent patriotism is taken to reconcile all animosities. They then proceed to consider the danger with which they are threatened, to settle the best plans for averting it, and to choose the generals who are to lead their armies against the common enemy. The first Gúrú-matá was assembled by Gúrú Góvind; and the latest was called in 1805, when the British army pursued Holkar into the Penjáb.[11]

Malcolm was, of course, exaggerating. Disinterested patriotism of the kind indicated in this passage is not what we find throughout the history of the Sikh misls. It is, however, no more than an exaggeration. There undoubtedly did exist a sense of unity which survived the departure of Ahmad Shāh Abdālī and the inter-misl conflicts which followed. Evasions and direct violations there may have been, and it appears that the gurmattā was not, in fact, used very often. These factors notwithstanding, the gurmattā nevertheless expressed a continuing sense of unity and did much to sustain it during a disintegrative phase.

The potency of the gurmattā lay in the belief that ultimate authority within the Panth belonged neither to popular opinion nor to the assembly of sardārs. Authority within the Panth had been retained by the eternal Gurū whose presence at the meeting was symbolized by the sacred scriptures. Although the actual decision may have been the product of the sardārs' debate the sanction attached to the decision was commonly stronger than the military power of any misl or combination of misls. The sanction lay in the conviction that the Gurū's will had been elicited and that once the decision had been reached opposition amounted to blasphemy, or even apostasy. This can be an exceedingly uncomfortable situation and we need have no diffi-

[11] John Malcolm, *Sketch of the Sikhs* (London, 1812), pp. 120–3. Reprinted in M. A. Macauliffe, H. H. Wilson, *et al.*, *The Sikh Religion: A Symposium* (Calcutta, 1958), pp. 121–2.

culty in understanding the reluctance encountered by latter-day attempts to revive the doctrine.

During the eighteenth century, however, this doctrine served the Panth well. Although essentially a military instrument which had evolved in response to a military need, it expressed in an unusually coherent form the more general religious doctrine of the Gurū's continuing presence within any congregation of his disciples. As such it fulfilled a useful cohesive role. Ironically, its very effectiveness was largely responsible for the suddenness of its decline when the need which had produced it no longer existed. The need passed when Rañjīt Siṅgh extinguished the misl system, replacing it with a strong and relatively centralized monarchy. It was this monarchy which now assumed the cohesive role. A Jaṭ Sikh of remarkable ability had established the *Khālsā Sarkār*, the rule of the Khālsā. The disintegrative tendency had been replaced by a strong impulse towards reintegration of the Panth.

In this situation the gurmattā could only be regarded as a positive hindrance. Corporate decisions bearing a religious sanction could hardly be welcome to Rañjīt Siṅgh in his effort to bring all other leaders under his own control and he eventually imposed a ban upon all but strictly religious assemblies. The gurmattā had, in practice, rarely been applied to strictly religious issues, for the eighteenth century had not provided conditions congenial to careful religious disputation. As a result the theory of the *Gurū Panth* quickly lapsed into disuse, leaving the issue of religious authority to the doctrine of a scriptural Gurū, the *Gurū Granth*. All other questions previously determined by reference to the corporate Gurū were meanwhile appropriated by Rañjīt Siṅgh and later by his British successors.

This leads us into the nineteenth century, but before leaving the eighteenth century we must take notice of the other important agent of Sikh cohesion which emerged during this period. Unlike the doctrine of the *Gurū Panth* this second agent has suffered no permanent eclipse. Although it did for a brief period show signs of receding it soon recovered its strength and to this day it accounts for the most obvious features of Sikh custom and conduct.

The other important cohesive institution which crystallized during the eighteenth century was the *rahat*, or *rahit*, the Sikh 'code of discipline'. To be more explicit we should refer to it as the Khālsā code of discipline, and the development which we shall now examine reflects the eighteenth-century evolution of the Khālsā brotherhood. Our attention will, however, be focused on the actual discipline of the brotherhood, for it is the discipline which embodies the cohesive ideals of the Khālsā.

As in the case of the question of authority we have here an issue which, according to tradition, was definitively settled by a pronouncement of Gurū Gobind Siṅgh, but which we can now see to have been, in part at least, the result of gradual growth during the course of the eighteenth century. Tradition declares that the promulgation of a binding code of discipline was a part of the Baisākhī Day proceedings in 1699, and that this code continues essentially unchanged to the present day. It is, however, clear from the *rahat-nāmās* of the eighteenth century (the recorded 'Codes of Discipline') that the conventions of the Khālsā were in the process of evolution during this period. The evidence is not substantial in volume, but it suggests that the question of the 'Five K's', for example, was not finally settled until well into the eighteenth century.[12]

The term 'Five K's' refers to the five symbols which must be worn by the Sikh who is a baptized member of the Khālsā. All begin with the letter 'k' and hence the collective term *pañj kakke*, or 'Five K's'. The five symbols are the *keś* (uncut hair), *kaṅghā* (comb), *kirpān* (dagger), *kaṛā* (steel bangle), and *kachh* (a pair of breeches which must not reach below the knees). Although the origins of these symbols should probably concern the anthropologist rather than the historian the latter can nevertheless make some observations concerning their inclusion in the agreed 'Code of Discipline' which finally issued from the eighteenth century.

There can be no doubt that the Five K's reflect the complex of Jaṭ cultural patterns and contemporary historical events which produced so many of the features now associated exclu-

[12] For a note on the *rahat-nāmā* see E. Trumpp, *The Adi Granth* (London, 1877), pp. cxiii-cxvi. Attar Singh of Bhadaur provided an early translation of two of the more important *rahat-nāmās* under the title *The Rayhit Nama of Pralad Rai or the Excellent Conversation of the Duswan Padsha and Nand Lal's Rayhit Nama or Rules for the Guidance of the Sikhs in Religious Matters* (Lahore, 1876). See also J. D. Cunningham, *A History of the Sikhs* (London, 1849), Appx. iv, pp. 372–7; Kānh Singh Nābhā, *Gurumat Sudhākar* (Amritsar, 1901), pp. 453–507; J. S. Grewal, *From Guru Nanak to Maharaja Ranjit Singh* (Amritsar, 1972), chap. XII.

sively with the Khālsā brotherhood. Uncut hair was a Jaṭ custom which during and prior to this period was evidently observed by Hindu and Muslim Jaṭs as well as by Sikh Jaṭs.[13] The bearing of arms, represented by the dagger, was also a Jaṭ practice and one which received ample encouragement from the events of the eighteenth century. With these two symbols may be paired the comb and the bangle respectively. The breeches are rather harder to understand in this context, but it seems safe to assume that this symbol must also relate in some way to the same situation.[14]

The same complex of Jaṭ culture and contemporary circumstances also accounts for the explicit prohibitions which find a place in the Khālsā discipline. In this case it was the pressure of contemporary events which provided the dominant influence. Whereas the prohibitions directed against the consumption of *halāl* meat and intercourse with Muslim women do not reflect a 1699 situation, they do most certainly accord well with the eighteenth-century struggle against the Mughals and, more particularly, against the Afghāns. The same situation presumably accounts also for the ban on the use of tobacco.

With the Five K's and other features of the Khālsā code of discipline these prohibitions were recorded in the evolving *rahat-nāmās*. These *rahat-nāmās* purported to record the actual instructions of the tenth Gurū and because their claim was accepted they acquired the sanction which was needed to enforce the code. To flout the *rahat* would be tantamount to disobeying the Gurū himself.

An enumeration of the Five K's and the specific prohibitions provides merely two of the more prominent features of the Khālsā discipline. More could be cited in support of the claim that the discipline evolved gradually during the course of the eighteenth century in response to inherited cultural patterns and the impact of contemporary events. Such features are of con-

[13] *The Commentary of Father Monserrate, S. J.*, trans. J. S. Hoyland, ed. S. N. Banerjee (London, 1922), p. 110. Waris Shah, *The Adventures of Hir and Ranjha*, trans. C. F. Usborne, ed. Mumtaz Hasan (Karachi, 1966), p. 30. Cf also the Mirzā-Sāhibān cycle. See Eng. trans., line 273, in R. C. Temple, *Legends of the Panjab*, Vol. 3 (Bombay and London, 1886), p. 23. See also comments by John Griffiths and William Francklin in Ganda Singh (ed.), *Early European Accounts of the Sikhs* (Calcutta, 1962), pp. 88, 105; and Charles Masson, *Narrative of Various Journeys in Balochistan &c.*, Vol. 1 (London, 1842), p. 434.

[14] For a fuller discussion by a social anthropologist see J. P. Singh Uberoi, 'On Being Unshorn', in *Sikhism and Indian Society* (Simla, 1967), pp. 87–100.

siderable interest and could be pursued at much greater length. The temptation must, however, be resisted, for in the pursuit we should soon lose sight of the cohesive function with which this essay is primarily concerned. The Khālsā code of discipline which crystallized during the eighteenth century has fulfilled this role with conspicuous success. With the passage of time certain amendments have inevitably been imposed upon the discipline, but with one exception these have been surprisingly insignificant. The exception is the distinctive turban. The turban itself is, of course, as old as the Sikh Panth and much older. What interests us here is the manner in which the turban has assumed, like the other symbols, a particular status. This is a development which still lacks the formal sanction attached to the ban on hair-cutting, but which during the nineteenth and twentieth centuries has been accorded an increasing importance in the endless quest for self-identification.

This carries us forward into the nineteenth and twentieth centuries. Two final developments should be noted before leaving the eighteenth century behind. One which has already been briefly mentioned is the elevation of Amritsar to the rank of first amongst the community's religious centres. Amritsar had briefly occupied this status during the period of Gurū Arjan (1581–1606) and it was there that the *Gurū Granth Sāhib* was compiled. When, however, Gurū Hargobind moved to the Śivālik Hills in 1634 Amritsar lost its primacy and did not recover it until almost a century had passed. Its subordinate status during this period is highlighted by the fact that Gurū Gobind Siṅgh never visited the town. It was only when the dispersed jathās and misls began to use it as a convenient meeting-place that its primacy was restored. This restored status it retained even when Rañjīt Siṅgh established his political capital in Lahore. As chief of the Sikh pilgrimage centres Amritsar has ever since played an important cohesive role. Within the city a particular focus for piety and panthic activity has been provided by the most famous of all Sikh shrines, the celebrated Golden Temple.

Finally, there is the emergence of a distinctive Sikh historiography, an essentially eighteenth-century product which in an amplified form endures to this day. The events of the eighteenth century provided abundant material to develop and sustain a particular image of the Khālsā. Born in tribulation and nurtured in persecution, the Khālsā triumphed over all. To this day the cry of the eighteenth-century Panth can evoke a powerful response: *rāj karegā khālsā*, 'the Khālsā shall rule!' This too has been a most effective agent of cohesion in Sikh history.

The political ideal serves to link the eighteenth and nineteenth centuries, for it was believed that the ideal had found fulfilment in the person of Mahārājā Rañjīt Siṅgh. As we have already seen, Rañjīt Siṅgh terminated the disorders of eighteenth-century Pañjāb by establishing a strong if short-lived monarchy. This kingdom was regarded as a fulfilment of the Khālsā ideal and for four decades the Panth suffered no serious lack of cohesion. Beliefs which were in plain contradiction to the Gurūs' teachings penetrated the community, but did nothing to undermine its sense of strength and unity. Even the struggles which broke out within the Khālsā following the death of Rañjīt Siṅgh in 1839 did not immediately affect this sense of identity. The real threat did not emerge until power and patronage passed to the British.

The final annexation of the Pañjāb by the British took place in 1849 and was followed by a marked recession in Sikh fortunes, particularly those of the rural Jaṭ Sikhs. Several decades of relative peace under Rañjīt Siṅgh had brought increasing population pressure in the fertile plains tract, and the disbanding of the Khālsā army further aggravated this condition. British observers were soon commenting on the signs of dissolution which they saw all around them and confidently predicted the total absorption of the Sikhs into 'the great ocean of Hinduism'.[15] To these observers it seemed clear that the collapse of Sikh political power had cancelled the primary advantage of Khālsā observance and that accordingly a total relapse must soon overwhelm the Panth.

The signs of dissolution were certainly present, but they were soon to be belied. The credit for the reintegration which confounded the prophets is commonly ascribed to the British army authorities who insisted that their Sikh recruits should retain the traditional symbols intact. Although this insistence was not

[15] W. H. Sleeman, *Rambles and Recollections of an Indian Official*, ed. V. A. Smith (Westminster, 1893), p. 128. See also the quotations from Major R. Leech's *Notes on the Religion of the Sikhs and Other Sects Inhabiting the Panjab* in N. Gerald Barrier, *The Sikhs and their Literature* (Delhi, 1970), p. xviii.

without its importance the popular interpretation certainly involves a misplacement of emphasis. The primary significance of the army policy was the economic opportunity which it afforded. Military employment was congenial to the Jaṭs and for those of the central tract it provided a welcome means of alleviating the increasing land and population pressure. The measure of economic revival offered by the opportunity was further stimulated by the success of the canal colonies. This economic revival was the real basis for the restoration of a strong panthic consciousness and for the insistence upon a return to the orthodox Khālsā symbols which accompanied it.

During the last three decades of the nineteenth century this restoration found expression in the Siṅgh Sabhās, a group of closely related Sikh organizations dedicated to religious, social, and educational reform.[16] The Siṅgh Sabhā movement must be seen both as a response to the disintegration which threatened the Panth during the middle years of the century and as an expression of the revival which followed this period. The ideal which it so vigorously promoted was essentially the backward look to a golden age. Panthic revival, according to this ideal, depended upon a return to the earlier vision of the Khālsā, to the customs and beliefs which had brought glory during the eighteenth century and which had since been permitted to decay. Three points of emphasis were of particular importance. There was, first, the exhortation to resume in its full rigour the code of discipline. Secondly, there was an insistence upon the paramount authority of the Gurū. And thirdly, there developed a sustained campaign to secure Khālsā control of the Sikh temples (the erstwhile dharamsālās, now known as gurdwaras). The slide towards disintegration was halted. Once again the Panth had recovered its sense of identity and purpose. An influx of outcastes created problems which to this day remain unsolved, but even this must be seen primarily as an example of the new *élan*. Such an influx would never have taken place during a period of recession.

The authority of the scripture (the *Gurū Granth Sāhib*) is a subject which will be more fully treated in the fourth essay.

[16] For accounts of the rise of the Siṅgh Sabhā Movement and of the associated Chief Khālsā Diwān see N. Gerald Barrier, op. cit., pp. xxiii–xlv. Also Khushwant Singh, *A History of the Sikhs*, Vol. 2 (Princeton, N.J., 1966), pp. 136–47; and Harbans Singh, *The Heritage of the Sikhs* (Bombay, 1964), pp. 138–47.

Here it will be sufficient to note its place in the sequence of cohesive ideals and institutions. During the period when the doctrine of the *Gurū Panth* was accorded a particular authority the way was being prepared for the ascendancy of the *Gurū Granth* by the custom of deciding all gurmattās in the presence of the scripture. Following Rañjīt Siṅgh's suppression of the Khālsā assemblies the scripture assumed the role, at least in theory, of primary religious authority. This authority it has never relinquished and to this day it serves as the focus not merely of Sikh devotion but also of Sikh loyalty to the Panth. It still survives in situations which permit a growing neglect of the Khālsā discipline.

The campaign for control of the gurdwaras was undertaken because many of these temples were in the hands of superintendents (*mahants*) who made no pretence of observing the Khālsā discipline. If the Siṅgh Sabhā reformation was to have any meaning it must obviously extend to the Panth's shrines and to the mahants who still commanded a measure of influence as instructors in the faith. This was the purpose of the agitation. Its function (and this is what interests us here) was to reunite the Panth through the pursuit of a common objective.

The agitation achieved its declared objective when in 1925 the Pañjāb Government approved the Sikh Gurdwaras Act. This provided for a committee (the Shiromaṇī Gurdwara Parbandhak Committee, or SGPC), largely elected by the Sikh constituency and controlling a substantial proportion of the Pañjāb gurdwaras.[17] The purpose had been achieved and so the agitation ceased. With it went a significant measure of the Panth's cohesion. An expanded historiography sustained it in some degree, and both the code of discipline and the scripture still retained (at least in theory) an unchallenged authority. There were, however, evident signs of another disintegrative phase, for the very success of the so-called Gurdwara Reform Movement had introduced fresh problems. These problems derived from the pattern of political activity established by the successful agitation and from the prize which now lay within the grasp of a political victor.

[17] Baldev Raj Nayar, *Minority Politics in the Punjab* (Princeton, N.J., 1966), p. 177. The SGPC had been constituted by the Sikhs in 1920. The 1925 Act accorded it official recognition.

The prize was control of the substantial funds received by gurdwaras throughout the Pañjāb and now entrusted to the SGPC. Many gurdwaras drew large incomes from their endowments and when pooled these incomes provided an impressive source of financial supply. This wealth ensured that the SGPC should become the principal focus of Sikh politics and many gurdwaras (particularly the Golden Temple) have in consequence become primary centres of political activity. Control of the SGPC is fiercely contested, for it confers immense powers of patronage. These contests are by no means confined to the formal quinquennial elections required by the Sikh Gurdwaras Act.[18] The Akālī Party (the Akālī Dal) has always won these elections and in all recent instances it has dominated the polls, routing its Congress and Communist rivals and securing a superficially strong majority.[19] The more acrimonious disputes have taken place *within* the dominant Akālī Dal.[20] This situation is scarcely conducive to panthic cohesion, except when a particular objective serves to sustain a temporary unity. As a result the Panth has, during recent years, manifested a bewildering succession of struggles for political power, and an insistent quest for new causes. This phase is still with us and governments which resist claims for statehood or the possession of Chaṇḍīgaṛh help to stay the forces of disintegration.

In terms of formal religious observance and personal piety the gurdwaras have provided, and continue to provide, a strong bond of panthic unity. All who visit them join in a common service of worship, singing together and eating the same food in the *laṅgar* (the refectory attached to every gurdwara). At another level, however, they have had a reverse effect. As

[18] The total statutory membership of the SGPC is 160. Of these 140 are elected quinquennially and the remainder are either nominated or sit *ex officio*. The electorate consists exclusively of male and female Sikhs living in the states of Pañjāb and Haryānā who are over twenty-one years of age and are not apostate (i.e. have not renounced the formal external symbols of the Sikh faith). Those eligible for election must be Sikhs over twenty-five, literate in Gurmukhī, and not apostate. Baldev Raj Nayar, op. cit., p. 177. Elections are currently long overdue, the term of the last SGPC having expired in January 1969.

[19] The Akālī, Congress, and Communist parties all sponsor candidates for both the Pañjāb state legislature and the SGPC. At both levels the Akālī membership is almost exclusively Sikh although the party vigorously claims to be non-communal.

[20] In recent years the most celebrated of these disputes has been the struggle between Master Tara Singh and Sant Fateh Singh. The latter, originally a protégé of Tara Singh, organized his own Akālī Dal in 1962 and in the same year succeeded in wresting control of the SGPC from his former mentor. Baldev Raj Nayar, op. cit., pp. 194–5.

centres of political activity they divide rather than unite. In many respects the gurdwara can be regarded as an epitome of the Panth's current condition. It provides a focus for genuine personal devotion and for a continuing loyalty to traditional forms; and at the same time it serves as an arena for disruptive political strife.

A brief recapitulation concludes this survey of the ideals and institutions which have successively served a cohesive role in the history of the Sikh Panth. The survey began with the person of Nānak, the first Gurū. In this earliest phase the necessary and sufficient bond was provided by direct personal loyalty to the acknowledged Master. The loyalty owed to Nānak was extended for a period of more than 150 years after his death by the line of nine successor Gurūs and by the circulation of janam-sākhīs. At the beginning of the eighteenth century the personal line became extinct with the death of Gurū Gobind Siṅgh. An attempt to continue the personal line having failed the doctrine of the *Gurū Panth* was elevated to supreme authority. This doctrine found its clearest expression in the gurmattā, or resolution of the Sarbat Khālsā.

Meanwhile another powerful agent of cohesion was evolving from inherited Jaṭ patterns and in direct response to contemporary circumstances. This was the Khālsā, and specifically the Khālsā code of discipline. Following the rise of Rañjīt Siṅgh the code continued to be observed, but the doctrine of the *Gurū Panth* made way for the ascending doctrine of the *Gurū Granth.* Disintegration followed annexation and was in turn followed by reintegration under the impulse of the Siṅgh Sabhās. Siṅgh Sabhā objectives were at first pursued through education, preaching, and literature. As the Akālī movement overtook them, however, emphasis shifted increasingly to political methods, notably to political agitation. Although education survived this shift and continues to occupy an important place in panthic policy, it is primarily through political action that the Panth of today seeks to maintain its cohesion.

4

THE SIKH SCRIPTURES

BOOKS which refer to the Sikh scriptures can be very confusing. A variety of titles are used and it is not always clear which work is being described or cited. For this reason it may be helpful to begin this description with a brief explanation of some of the titles which one must inevitably encounter in an examination of the Sikh sacred scriptures. The scriptures of the Sikhs are not limited to a single volume, although it is true that one collection is accorded a particular degree of sanctity. Confusion can arise because this primary scripture has more than one standard title, and also because there are other scriptures which must be carefully distinguished from it.

The primary scripture is variously referred to as the *Granth Sāhib*, the *Gurū Granth Sāhib*, the *Ādi Granth*, or as an expanded combination of the latter two. *Granth* simply means 'book'. To this the honorific *Sāhib* is affixed to designate sanctity, and *Gurū* is normally prefixed as an indication of the status now attached to this particular scripture. In the third essay reference was made to the manner in which the gap left by the death of Gurū Gobind Singh was filled first by the doctrine of the *Gurū Panth* and then later by the doctrine of the *Gurū Granth.* To both the body of believers (*panth*) and to the scripture (*granth*) there was accorded the authority previously exercised by the personal Gurū. Each thereby acquired the title which designated this status and it is as the *Gurū Granth Sāhib* that this primary scripture is most commonly known.[1]

The alternative title *Ādi Granth* tends to be confined to learned discussion. *Ādi* means 'first' or 'original', and is used to distinguish this first scripture of the Sikhs from their second scripture, the *Dasam Granth* or 'Book of the Tenth (Gurū)'. Although in its brief form this title is restricted in use it does appear frequently in conjunction with the more popular title. *Ādi Srī Gurū*

[1] The additional honorific *srī*, *sirī*, or *śrī* may also be prefixed to give *Srī Gurū Granth Sāhib.*

Granth Sāhib is the standard title for published editions of the scripture.

An examination of the *Ādi Granth* will occupy the greater portion of this essay. It will be followed by a brief description of the *Dasam Granth* and finally by an even briefer notice of the remaining works which can legitimately be regarded as sacred scripture. These are the poetic works of Bhāī Gurdās and Nand Lāl Goyā, and the narrative janam-sākhīs which provided the topic of the second essay.

According to tradition the *Ādi Granth*, or *Gurū Granth Sāhib*, was compiled by the fifth Gurū, Arjan, during the years A.D. 1603–4. To this extent the tradition appears to be well founded. A manuscript bearing the latter date is still extant and there is no sufficient reason to doubt its authenticity. Tradition also provides an explanation for Gurū Arjan's decision to compile this collection of hymns. It is said that his enemies (notably the Mīṇās led by Prithī Chand) were circulating spurious works bearing the name of Nānak in order to seduce the Sikhs from their loyalty to the legitimate succession. In order to combat this threat to his authority Gurū Arjan decided to prepare an authorized text bearing his own imprimatur.

Having reached this decision the Gurū established a camp in Amritsar during the year 1603 and there ordered a tank to be dug. Upon completion it was named Rāmsar and beside this tank he supervised the compilation of his authorized version. Hymns selected by the Gurū were dictated to his amanuensis Bhāī Gurdās and the bulky work was finally completed during the late summer of 1604. It was then installed in Harimandir, the principal Sikh shrine widely known in its present form as the Golden Temple.[2]

Gurū Arjan's principal source was a similar collection which tradition attributes to the third Gurū, Amar Dās. This collection consisted of two volumes, the so-called Goindvāl *pothīs*. These volumes included the works of the first three Gurūs together with those of the *bhagats*,[3] and so provided a substan-

[2] The temple is also commonly called Darbār Sāhib. This is the title generally used by Sikhs today. The term Golden Temple is largely confined to Europeans and to English-language sources.

[3] *bhagat*, or *bhakta*, literally 'follower of *bhagti* (*bhakti*)', 'devotee'. Both words are normally used as titles of respect and are applied to the more distinguished of the later medieval *bhakti* poets. Kabīr, who in Hindī tradition is referred to as Bhakta Kabīr (or Sant Kabīr), is in Sikh usage invariably known as Bhagat Kabīr.

tial nucleus. The actual copying of the volumes had been done by Sahansrām, a grandson of Gurū Amar Dās, and at the time when Gurū Arjan decided to prepare a second collection the two volumes were in the possession of Mohan, the elder son of Amar Dās and father of Sahansrām. Bābā Mohan (so the tradition continues) had not approved of his father's choice of Rām Dās as fourth Gurū, and so Arjan, the son of Rām Dās, had some difficulty in persuading him to part with the manuscript. His objections were overcome only when Arjan went in person to Goindvāl and sang a song in praise of him outside his window. Touched by the compliment, Mohan agreed to give the volumes on loan. They were carried with great reverence to Amritsar on a palanquin and subsequently returned in the same manner.

Although certain features of the tradition may arouse some suspicion,[4] there seems to be no doubt that the two volumes did in fact exist and that Gurū Arjan utilized them for his own collection. Two volumes purporting to be the original Goindvāl *pothīs* are still extant, or were extant until recently. If they do in fact still exist their precise location is uncertain, but descriptions left by the late Bābā Prem Siṅgh of Hoti support the claims which are made on their behalf.[5]

The Goindvāl volumes can thus be regarded as a first recension of the *Ādi Granth* and Gurū Arjan's collection as an enlarged second recension. To the nucleus which they provided he added the numerous works which he had himself composed, those of his father Gurū Rām Dās, and a small number by contemporary *bhagats*. Very few of the latter can have been included in this manner, for almost all of the *bhagat bāṇī* is said to be included in the Goindvāl volumes.

A considerable mystery surrounds the history of the actual manuscript which Bhāī Gurdās is said to have written at Gurū Arjan's dictation. The Soḍhī family of Kartārpur in Jullundur District possess the manuscript which is regarded as the original work of Bhāī Gurdās and, as we shall see later, there is sound reason for accepting this claim. But how did it find its way to Kartārpur? Once again we are compelled to fall back on the

[4] The story of Gurū Arjan's song under Mohan's window is plainly apocryphal. The hymn which he is supposed to have sung (*Gauṛī Chhant* 2, *Ādi Granth*, p. 248) does indeed use the word Mohan, but the context leaves no doubt that it is God who is being addressed by this name.

[5] Jodh Singh, *Srī Karatārpurī Bīṛ de Daraśan* (Patiala, 1968), pp. 123–5.

kind of tradition which, because it comes so much later than the actual events, must be treated with some caution. It is said that the sixth Gurū, Hargobind, kept the manuscript not in Harimandir but in his own house. From there it was stolen by his grandson Dhīr Mal who evidently intended that it should buttress his claims to the succession as Gurū. Some thirty years later followers of the ninth Gurū recovered it, but were instructed by their Master to return it. This was done by placing it in the Satluj River, from where Dhīr Mal recovered it miraculously unharmed. Gurū Gobind Siṅgh is said to have subsequently asked for it back and, when his request was refused, to have dictated another copy from memory.

From this point onwards even tradition fails to offer any coherent account of the manuscript's movements. The obvious conclusion is that throughout the eighteenth century it must have remained with Dhīr Mal's family, the Soḍhīs of Kartārpur. There are, however, fragments of tradition which indicate that this is not necessarily a safe conclusion. Not until 1849 does it emerge from obscurity. In that year, following the annexation of the Pañjāb, the volume together with its golden stand was discovered by the British in the custody of the Lahore court. An application was received from Soḍhi Sādhū Siṅgh of Kartārpur and in 1850 the volume was restored to him. Soḍhī Sādhū Siṅgh, 'out of respect and deference to the British Government', subsequently arranged for a copy to be made and presented to Queen Victoria.[6]

During the first two and a half centuries of its existence possession of the manuscript, though naturally something to be highly prized, was not an issue of prime importance. The doctrine of the scriptural Gurū had not yet been accorded the exclusive authority which it was later to acquire and current needs could be adequately served by the numerous copies (both complete and in part) which were in circulation. The significant change came with the rise of the Siṅgh Sabhā and, at almost the same time, the arrival of the printing press. The Siṅgh Sabhā reformers laid an insistent emphasis upon the absolute authority of the scripture, and the printing press pro-

[6] Nahar Singh (comp.), *Documents relating to Guru Gobind Singh's Swords and Sacred Books of the Sikhs in England* (Nangal Khurd, 1967), pp. 31, 36–7. The copy presented to Queen Victoria is now in the India Office Library (MSS. Panj. E2).

vided them with the means of disseminating it. Copies of the complete volume, with a standard text and pagination, have for many years been readily available and few Sikh families are without at least a *guṭkā* (a selection of the more important portions of the *Ādi Granth,* together with some extracts from the *Dasam Granth*).[7]

And yet, even today, the quest for a definitive authorized version is still not quite over. The final decision has been continually postponed by minor textual issues and by conflicting claims relating to the authenticity of the *Rāg-mālā* (the brief work which concludes the collection). In 1953 the Shiromaṇī Gurdwara Parbandhak Committee had blocks prepared for printing, but the completion of the work was indefinitely postponed by a dispute concerning the correct order of invocation and *rāg* title.[8] A decision was reached in 1962, but the actual printing of the approved version is evidently still pending.

To the outsider the points at issue may appear thoroughly insignificant and scarcely a sufficient reason for delaying the official version for so long. The orthodox Sikh, however, sees it differently. There may be some truth in the claim that a booksellers' lobby is hampering the work in the interests of unsold stock, but this is by no means the only obstructive element. To appreciate the problem it is necessary to understand something of the veneration in which a Sikh holds his scripture.

Perhaps the best method of acquiring this understanding is to visit the Golden Temple in Amritsar during the early hours of the morning. Numerous foreigners include Amritsar in their travel itineraries for the express purpose of seeing the Golden Temple, and then rob their visit of much of its potential value by going there during office hours. The truly interesting activity at the Golden Temple (or at any other gurdwara in India) is largely confined to the early morning and late evening. The best time to arrive is when the Temple opens at 3 a.m. If this can be managed the rewards are considerable, and amongst other things one can witness the daily installation of the *Gurū Granth Sāhib.*

No one observing this event could possibly mistake the degree

[7] The *Ardās,* or 'Sikh Prayer', is also commonly included. See below, pp. 65–6.

[8] For the meaning and importance of *rāg* in the *Ādi Granth* context see below, p. 71.

of reverence which is bestowed upon the Book. It is, indeed, a little unnerving, for it demonstrates with abundant clarity that he who seeks a deeper understanding must assuredly find himself treading upon unusually sacred ground. The volume is greeted with affectionate reverence because for the Sikhs of today it is the Gurū. The same spirit which successively inhabited the bodies of ten men is now believed to dwell in this particular Book. This is no mere fundamentalism of the Western variety. The Book is endued with a personality in the literal sense of that word. Through it the Gurū speaks to his followers in the same manner that he spoke to them while present in the flesh. Let us hasten to add that this is not the same as bibliolatry and the Sikh quite rightly rejects the suggestion that his belief necessarily involves *worship* of the *Gurū Granth Sāhib*. The Gurū, while in human form, expressly disclaimed this right, insisting that worship was due to God alone. If the human Gurū was not to be worshipped, then neither is the scriptural Gurū.

It is of vital importance that the student of Sikh religion and society should appreciate the depth of this reverence, just as he should understand the offence which can be caused by the use of tobacco in the presence of orthodox Sikhs. The odium which in Sikh circles still attaches to the name of Ernst Trumpp derived in no small measure from his culpable insensitivity in this respect. During a visit to Amritsar he made the disastrous mistake of smoking a cigar while consulting a copy of the *Gurū Granth Sāhib*.[9] The *giānīs* who observed him doing so were, needless to say, outraged and the incident is remembered to this day. There may be signs of disintegration evident within the community today, but an obvious decline in reverence for the scripture is not one of them.

The place where most foreigners will observe a copy of the *Gurū Granth Sāhib* is in a gurdwara or, to be more precise, in a public gurdwara. Strictly speaking, any room which contains a copy is thereby constituted a gurdwara and Sikh families who can afford the extra room commonly set one aside as a family gurdwara. This will normally contain little except the

[9] The incident was described by M. A. Macauliffe in a published lecture entitled *The Sikh Religion and its Advantages to the State* (Simla, 1903), p. 2. Reprinted in M. A. Macauliffe, H. H. Wilson, *et al.*, *The Sikh Religion: A Symposium* (Calcutta, 1958), p. 1. This misleadingly titled book should not be confused with Macauliffe's six-volume work *The Sikh Religion* (Oxford, 1909).

sacred volume set in an elevated position. If the worshippers are to sit on the floor a low dais will serve the purpose. This is invariably the case in the Pañjāb itself, but in England chairs are sometimes used and in consequence the elevation of the volume has to be raised. The book will always be draped (normally in expensive cloth) and will commonly lie beneath a canopy. While it is undraped it is usually protected by the use of a fly-whisk. Whenever it has to be moved it should be carried on the head, and if being transported along a road some form of advance warning should be given in order to ensure that the people who witness its passing may show proper respect. On festival days a copy, mounted on a truck or bus and properly protected, will figure prominently in the customary procession.[10]

Within the structure of Sikh worship the *Gurū Granth Sāhib* is central in much more than a merely physical sense. All aspects of Sikh worship relate directly to it and practically the entire content of all worship is drawn from it. Many visit the gurdwara simply for *darśan*, or 'audience', with the *Gurū Granth Sāhib*. This consists of entering the gurdwara, prostrating oneself before the Book, making an offering, and accepting *praśād*[11] from the *granthī* ('reader') responsible for the care of the volume. Even when a formal service is in progress this is a common pattern. The formal service consists almost entirely of singing hymns from the scripture. Groups of three singers (*rāgīs*) lead the congregation and those present may, if they wish, join in hymns which they know. A garland may be offered and in return there may be given a garland, previously offered, which has meanwhile been in close proximity to the sacred volume. When the flowers wither the proper method of disposal is to cast the garland on flowing water.

The only important exceptions to the rule of drawing exclusively from the *Ādi Granth* are, first, the occasional use of selections from the other approved scriptures; and secondly, the regular recitation of *Ardās*, the so-called Sikh Prayer. The *Ardās*

[10] For a description of the modern gurdwara and its place in Sikh life, both in the Pañjāb and in England, see Alan G. James, *Sikh Children in Britain* (London, 1974), pp. 35 ff, 64.

[11] The sacramental food distributed at temples, both Hindu and Sikh. The Sikh variety (consisting of equal parts of coarsely refined wheat flour, sugar, and *ghī*) is distinguished by the name *kaṛāh praśād*. See p. 87.

(literally 'Petition') is an unusually interesting text which, because it evolved during the eighteenth century, expresses with unusual clarity the ideals of that period. Earlier forms evidently concluded with an exhortation to accept the Panth as Gurū.[12] The version currently in use concludes with a similar exhortation to acknowledge the *Gurū Granth Sāhib*. The concluding passage is worth quoting, for no words are more familiar to a Sikh and none express with greater clarity the doctrine of the spiritual Gurū embodied in the scripture.

āgiān bhaī akāl kī
tabī chalāio panth
sab sikhān kau hukam hai
gurū mānio granth
gurū granth jī mānio
paragaṭ gurān kī deh
jā kā hiradā sudh hai
khoj śabad men leh

From the Timeless One there came the bidding,
In accordance with which was established the Panth.
To all Sikhs there comes this command:
Acknowledge as Gurū the *Granth*.
Acknowledge the *Granth* as Gurū,
For it is the manifest body of the Masters.
Ye whose hearts are pure,
Seek Him in the Word!

The prominence accorded the *Gurū Granth Sāhib* in regular gurdwara worship extends to all other Sikh ceremonies. The passages which the devout Sikh should recite in the morning and evening are taken from it. When he is married he circumambulates the sacred volume instead of the sacred fire, and when he is cremated the ceremony is performed in its presence. Before he proceeds to his daily labours he may 'take a command' from the scripture. This custom consists of opening the volume at random and reading the composition which appears at the top of the left-hand page. The passage which is turned up in this manner is believed to bestow a specific guidance for that particular day. A similar procedure is followed when choosing a name for a child. Once again the *Gurū Granth Sāhib* is opened

[12] E. Trumpp, op. cit., p. cxv, n. 2.

at random and the first letter at the top of the left-hand page must be the first letter of the chosen name.

The custom of taking daily guidance by means of a random opening may also be extended to provide a public oracle. Perhaps the most dramatic instance of using the scripture for this purpose was an event which took place in 1920. This was the period of the so-called mass movement when substantial numbers of Pañjābī outcastes, in quest of an enhanced social status, were joining either the Christian Church or the Khālsā. The Church, because it had previously been so tiny in the Pañjāb, suffered no serious dislocation, but for the much larger Khālsā the consequent problems were considerable. Inevitably the crisis assumed its most acute form over the issue of commensality, and specifically the question of whether or not converts from outcaste groups could offer and receive sacramental food (*kaṛāh praśād*) at the gurdwaras. A small group of Siṅgh Sabhā reformers advocated their right to do so and could point to passages in the scripture which supported their claim. The burden of tradition is, however, heavy and the prohibitions which obstructed a total acceptance of outcaste converts could not be so easily cast aside.

The issue came to a head in 1920 following a baptismal convention held in Amritsar. These conventions resembled the *śudhī* ceremonies of the Ārya Samāj in that they were held for the purpose of initiating outcastes, and on this occasion there had been the usual baptism of new converts into the Khālsā. But could these outcaste converts proceed to the Golden Temple in the expectation that they would there be permitted to offer and receive *kaṛāh praśād*? The administrators of the Golden Temple had already made it abundantly clear that they would be refused. The conference members nevertheless proceeded in procession to the Golden Temple and lodged their demand. This was again refused and it appeared that a serious disturbance might develop. Eventually it was agreed that the Gurū should be consulted and that his decision should be binding. With due ceremony the sacred volume was opened at random and revealed a passage which, it was maintained, put the issue beyond all doubt.

niguṇiā no āpe bakhasi lae bhāī satigur kī sevā lāi
satigur kī sevā utam hai bhāī rām nāmi chitu lāi

hari jīu āpe bakhasi milāi
guṇ hīṇ ham aparādhī bhāī pūrai satiguri lae ralāi

Upon the worthless He bestows His grace, brother, if
they will serve the True Gurū.
Exalted is the service of the True Gurū, brother, to
hold in remembrance the divine Name.
God Himself offers grace and mystic union.
Worthless sinners are we, brother, yet the True Gurū
has drawn us to that blissful union.[13]

Surely the words *niguṇiā* and *aparādhī* must embrace these lowly converts who had so recently declared their intention of seeking the Gurū's grace. The discomfited *sevādārs* withdrew in ignominy, leaving the triumphant reformers to dispense the *kaṛāh praśād*.[14]

One last ceremony to be noted is the *akhaṇḍ pāṭh*, or 'unbroken reading', a custom which tends to be restricted to the wealthier members of the Panth. An *akhaṇḍ pāṭh* is held in honour of a special occasion, as a special thanksgiving, as a supplication for some particular blessing, or as a means of averting a threatened disaster. A wedding will commonly be preceded by an *akhaṇḍ pāṭh* and likewise the opening of a new business. The return of a son from overseas may warrant one and for some it will be regarded as a wise precaution in the event of a serious illness. For the reading a team of readers is assembled and relieving each other in turn they intone the entire scripture without a break. This takes two days. Anyone may sit and listen at any time, and all who are involved in the occasion which prompted the ceremony will gather before the sacred volume as the reading approaches its conclusion (*bhog*). In the principal gurdwaras an endless chain of unbroken reading is maintained, and in smaller temples they may be performed as a prelude to important festivals. One finds throughout the Pañjāb that the invention of the loud-speaker has enabled the promoters of these readings to share their benefits with the wider community. The custom is a recent entrant into Sikh tradition (possibly derived from the Hindu *yajña*) and is by no means universally accepted within the Panth.

[13] Gurū Amar Dās, *Soraṭh Dutukī* 2, *Ādi Granth*, p. 638.
[14] Teja Singh, *Essays in Sikhism* (Lahore, 1944), pp. 168–9.

The centrality of the *Gurū Granth Sāhib* in Sikh custom, and the manifold uses to which it is put, leave no room for doubt concerning its enormous importance to the Panth. Before leaving this aspect of the subject let it again be stressed that the function of this customary usage is of fundamental importance. This function, as we have already seen, is the maintenance of the Panth's cohesion.

We turn now to the contents of the *Ādi Granth*—to its language, its script, its structure, and its dominant theme. Macauliffe must bear most of the responsibility for the misleading impression that the language of the *Ādi Granth* is unusually difficult. Having listed a number of other scriptures he continues:

> The languages in which the holy writings of these religions are enshrined, though all difficult, are for the most part homogeneous, and after preliminary study with tutors can generally be mastered by the aid of grammars and dictionaries; but not so the mediaeval Indian dialects in which the sacred writings of the Sikh Gurus and Saints were composed. Hymns are found in Persian, mediaeval Prakrit, Hindi, Marathi, old Panjabi, Multani, and several local dialects. In several hymns the Sanskrit and Arabic vocabularies are freely drawn upon.[15]

As a pioneer Macauliffe encountered difficulties which will account for this judgement. It is, however, far from accurate. Although there is diversity in the language of the *Ādi Granth* this feature is by no means as pronounced as Macauliffe claimed and in practice presents relatively few problems once the Gurmukhī script has been mastered. Most of the elements which seem to suggest a heterogeneous collection of linguistic forms are, in reality, closely related. There are certainly words from such diverse languages as Sindhī, Arabic, Persian, and Marāṭhī, but with very rare exceptions these provide no more than vocabulary problems. They do not affect the essentially homogeneous structure of the *Ādi Granth* language. A knowledge of Hindī and Pañjābī is the basic requirement. With this equipment one can proceed with relative ease to a study of Sādhukaṛī, or Sant Bhāṣā, a medium employed all over northern India by religious poets of the fifteenth and sixteenth centuries.

[15] M. A. Macauliffe, *The Sikh Religion*, Vol. 1, p. v.

Within this general pattern the different Gurūs and bhagats made different linguistic emphases. Gurū Nānak's language normally has a strong Pañjābī colouring, although in a few cases he drew heavily from the vocabulary of a different language. Gurū Aṅgad and Gurū Rām Dās are also predominantly Pañjābī. Gurū Amar Dās, however, shows more signs of Braj influence, and in the case of Gurū Arjan the Braj emphasis is pronounced.

One mistake which Macauliffe avoided, but which other foreigners have commonly made, is to apply the title Pañjābī to the script which is used in the *Ādi Granth*. The term Pañjābī applies to the actual language, whereas the script is Gurmukhī (literally 'from the mouth of the Gurū'). Tradition claims it to be an invention of the second Gurū. Although this cannot be strictly accurate, its name and its early association with the works of the Gurūs suggest that its development (as opposed to its actual origins) must be intimately connected with the rise of the Sikh Panth. As the vehicle of the sacred scriptures it has acquired a sanctity of its own. It is an exceedingly simple script—even simpler than the Deva-nāgrī script to which it is closely related.

Another distinctive feature of the *Ādi Granth* is the unusually systematic arrangement of its contents. Within it we find a complex and generally consistent pattern of division and subdivision. The first of these is a threefold division into an introductory section, main text, and epilogue. The introductory section consists of works which had evidently acquired a liturgical usage. It opens with the celebrated *Japjī* of Gurū Nānak, a work which must rank as one of the most difficult in the entire scripture but which is nevertheless regarded as its quintessence. It is this composition, running to thirty-eight lengthy stanzas, which devout Sikhs are expected to repeat from memory every morning. The remainder of this opening section comprises fourteen hymns which are used as set forms of devotion for other times of the day. All fourteen are repeated elsewhere in the scripture.

The epilogue consists exclusively of miscellaneous works which could not be accommodated in the main text. These include collections of shaloks (couplets) attributed to Kabīr and Sheikh Farīd, panegyrics in praise of the Gurūs, and at the very end the puzzling *Rāg-mālā* which is evidently intended to summarize the various *rāgs* used in the main text.[16]

The *rāgs* provide the primary subdivision of the main text. Immediately after the introductory section comes *Sirī Rāg*. Within this section have been recorded all the works composed in this particular *rāg* which find a place in the volume. Next comes *Mājh*, then *Gauṛī*, then *Āsā*, and so on through a total of thirty-nine *rāgs*, concluding with *Jaijavantī*.

Each *rāg* is itself subdivided into several categories. First come the *chaupad* hymns (four brief stanzas with refrain), then the *aṣṭapadī* (eight stanzas with refrain), and then the *chhant*.[17] Next come works by the Gurūs which are in the appropriate metre, but which by reason of their greater length do not fit the earlier categories. These include Gurū Nānak's *Dakhaṇī Oaṅkār* and his *Sidh Goṣṭ*, both in the *Rāmakalī* measure; and Gurū Arjan's *Sukhmaṇī* in the *Gauṛī* measure. Still within the same *rāg* these longer works are followed by *vārs*, composite works consisting of a series of stanzas (*pauṛī*) each with attached shaloks. The stanzas of any particular *vār* are always the work of a single Gurū, but the shaloks (which are grouped in small clusters and prefixed to the stanzas) may be by different authors.

Finally, at the conclusion of each *rāg*, there is recorded the *bhagat bāṇī*, the compositions of various bhagats which, because they accorded with his own beliefs, had found a place in Gurū Amar Dās's earlier collection. Kabīr is the most prominent of the bhagats, followed by Nāmdev and Ravidās (Raidās). Two Sūfīs are included. Four hymns are attributed to Sheikh Farīd (in addition to the 117 shaloks recorded in the epilogue) and two to a lesser figure named Bhīkhaṇ. A single hymn is attributed to the celebrated Rāmānand.

The next subdivision takes place within the *chaupad*, *aṣṭapadī*, and *chhant*. These are arranged in a sequence which corresponds to the succession of Gurūs. The works of Gurū Nānak come first, and then those of Gurū Aṅgad, Gurū Amar Dās, Gurū Rām Dās, and Gurū Arjan respectively. All five Gurūs

[16] *rāg* (*rāga*): melodic organization. Any given *rāg* specifies particular notes to be used against the drone. Tradition and long usage have endowed each *rāg* with its own spiritual significance.

[17] *chhant* (Hindi *chhand*): lit. poem, song. In the *Ādi Granth* the term designates a hymn longer than a *chaupad* but shorter than an *aṣṭapadī*. Most examples consist of four stanzas, each comprising six lines.

styled themselves Nānak in their compositions,[18] but the differences of authorship are clearly distinguished by the use of the word *mahalā* with a figure corresponding to the Gurū's place in the succession. *Mahalā 1* precedes all of the compositions of Gurū Nānak, *Mahalā 2* those of Gurū Aṅgad, and so on through to *Mahalā 5* for the works of Gurū Arjan.[19]

Although this is not quite the end of the *Ādi Granth* system of classification, it must suffice for our present purpose. Not every *rāg* includes all of the categories just mentioned, but wherever they do occur they are almost always recorded in the sequence described above. Very few exceptions to this rule can be found and only one warrants a specific reference. There is a hymn by Kabīr which appears in the midst of a Gurū Arjan cluster, and which includes an unusually explicit rejection of both Hindu and Muslim authority.

> *nā ham hindū nā musalamān*
> *alah rām ke piṇḍ parān.*

> I am neither Hindu nor Muslim.
> (The One) Allah-Rām is the breath of my body.

The exception is worth noting because several writers, following Macauliffe, have accepted the hymn as the work of Gurū Arjan. This is probably incorrect, for an analogue appears in the *Kabīr-granthāvalī* tradition, and even in its *Ādi Granth* version it bears the name of Kabīr.[20]

The message of the *Ādi Granth* can be summarized very briefly. As in the case of its language we find beneath its superficial diversity a considerable degree of homogeneity. The Gurūs make one fundamental declaration. This they express in a wide variety of ways, building around it a coherent system of religious thought. The message is simply this: salvation is to be obtained through meditation on the divine Name. To recast this in terms which are perhaps more meaningful to a Western understand-

[18] In accordance with the standard procedure of Indian poetics the Gurūs incorporated their name in the last line or couplet of every composition. In every instance the name is Nānak. See above, p. 39.

[19] There are very few compositions attributed to *Mahalā 2* (Gurū Aṅgad). The standard text also includes some compositions attributed to Gurū Tegh Bahādur (*Mahalā 9*) and a couplet attributed to Gurū Gobind Siṅgh. See below, p. 75. The abbreviation *M* is frequently used in place of the word *mahalā* (*M1*, *M2*, etc.).

[20] *Bhairau* 5–3 (*Ādi Granth*, p. 1136) and *Kabīr-granthāvalī* 338 (Das version). Kabīr's *Bhairau* 12 (*Ādi Granth*, p. 1160) is also headed *Mahalā 5* (i.e. Gurū Arjan).

ing we can say that salvation is obtained by means of regular, persistent, disciplined meditation on the manifold expressions of the divine presence in the physical world and in human experience. It cannot be too strongly emphasized that the *Ādi Granth* is a collection of *religious* writings and that everything it contains relates directly to its soteriological concern.

The features which have been described above give an impression of order and clarity. In a general sense this impression is accurate and there can be few scriptures which possess a structure as consistent as that of the *Ādi Granth*. There are, however, certain aspects which are far from clear. The *Ādi Granth* is by no means without its problems (notably its textual problems) and some attention must now be directed to the more important of these issues.

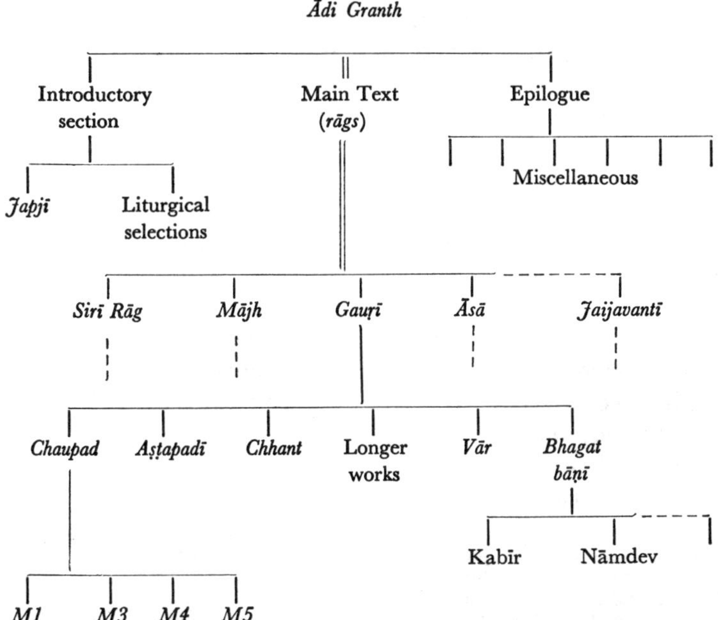

Structure of the *Ādi Granth*

The chief problem concerning the *Ādi Granth* arises from the fact that there is not one single version, but rather three different versions plus a number of variants. The variants can be disregarded in this discussion, but some attention must be directed to the three major versions. If the analysis succeeds only in muddying the water we must reply that a measure of obscurity is no more than an accurate representation of the present condition of our understanding.

Reference has already been made to the first of the three principal versions. This is the manuscript which, according to tradition, was written by Bhāī Gurdās at the dictation of Gurū Arjan, and which is now in the possession of the Soḍhīs of Kartārpur. It is variously known as the Kartārpur version, the Bhāī Gurdās version, or the *Ādi Bīṛ*. Unfortunately it is not possible to gain access to the manuscript. Although it is put on display once a month, no one is actually permitted to come close to the volume. The most one can do is to view it from afar and prostrate oneself before it. The only people who in recent years have been able to examine it are the few who were able to take advantage of a legal dispute during the mid-1940s. Believing that the manuscript should be the property of the Panth as a whole the Shiromaṇī Gurdwara Parbandhak Committee challenged the Soḍhī family's right of possession and during the course of the litigation permission to consult the volume could be secured from the Commissioner of Jullundur Division. The Soḍhī family eventually won the case, but at least some useful notes were recorded by three of the people who had meanwhile secured access to the manuscript.[21] One feature of particular significance is the fact that in some places the original text has been obliterated by the application of green ink (*haṛtāl*).

The second version is variously referred to as the Banno (or Bhāī Banno) version, the Māṅgaṭ version, or the *Khārī Bīṛ*. The adjective *khārī*, literally 'brackish' or 'bitter', means in this context 'spurious' or 'apocryphal'.[22] Two traditions exist con-

[21] The three were Dr. Jodh Singh, Dr. J. C. Archer, and Dr. C. H. Loehlin. Dr. Jodh Singh's observations are set out in detail in his *Srī Karatārpurī Bīṛ de Daraśan*, and briefly in an English article entitled 'A Note on Kartarpur Granth' published in *Proceedings of the Punjab History Conference*, First Session (Patiala: Punjabi University, 1966 for 1965), pp. 97–9. Professor Archer recorded his experience in an article entitled 'The Bible of the Sikhs', published in *The Review of Religion*, January 1949, pp. 115–25. Dr. Loehlin's account is to be found in his *The Sikhs and their Book* (Lucknow, 1946), pp. 44–5, and more recently in an article 'A Westerner looks at the Kartarpur Granth' published in *Proceedings of the Punjab History Conference*, First Session, pp. 93–6.

[22] It has been claimed that the name derives from Kharā, said to be an earlier name of Māṅgaṭ village. See Shamsher Singh Ashok, *Bhāī Banno jī te Khāre vālī bīṛ*,

cerning the origin of this version. According to one, Bhāī Banno, a resident of Māṅgaṭ village in District Gujrāt, visited Gurū Arjan and having developed a great interest in the new scripture asked permission to take it back to Māṅgaṭ on loan. Gurū Arjan was understandably loath to accede to the request, but eventually gave his permission on condition that Banno kept it at his village for one night only. Banno circumvented this condition by travelling very slowly to and from Māṅgaṭ. The lengthy journey afforded him time to make a copy of the volume without breaking his promise. The other tradition holds that he was entrusted with the responsibility of taking the original to Lahore for binding and he made his copy while on this mission.[23]

The third version has been briefly noticed in the account given above of the Kartārpur manuscript. Gurū Gobind Siṅgh, having been refused the latter, is said to have dictated his own copy from memory, adding to the original text fifty-nine hymns and fifty-six couplets of his father, Gurū Tegh Bahādur, and also one couplet of his own. Quite apart from the feat of memory the tradition is inaccurate, for the works of Gurū Tegh Bahādur had already been incorporated in at least one version which predates the period of Gurū Gobind Siṅgh.[24] This is, however, of small importance. The significant facts are, first, that a version incorporating this extra material did become current; and secondly, that apart from extra material it corresponds closely to the Kartārpur manuscript. This is the Damdamā version, so called because Gurū Gobind Siṅgh is said to have dictated it while staying at the village of Damdamā Sāhib.[25] Modern printed copies follow this third text in including the works of Gurū Tegh Bahādur and the couplet attributed to Gurū Gobind Siṅgh.

The problem which confronts us arises from a comparison of the Kartārpur and Banno versions. We note, in the first

in *Khoj Patrikā* (Patiala), no. 4, May 1970, pp. 36–7. Ashok's article gives a traditional account of the life of Banno.

[23] M. A. Macauliffe, op. cit., Vol. 3, p. 66.

[24] Khushwant Singh claims there are two such versions (op. cit., Vol. 1, p. 93, n. 35).

[25] Bhaṭinda District. The village is also known by its earlier name Talvaṇḍī. Sābo, or Sābo kī Talvaṇḍī. The name was changed in honour of the occasion when Gurū Gobind Siṅgh made the village his resting-place (*damdamā*), i.e. when he spent a period there following the Battle of Muktsar in 1705.

place, that the claim to originality made on behalf of the Kartārpur manuscript appears to be sound. Dr. Jodh Singh has argued this in a manner which seems to be entirely convincing.[26] At first sight, however, this manuscript appears to be an exception to the general run of early manuscripts which, until well into the eighteenth century, are almost always Banno texts or variants of it. And, as we have just observed, the Banno version is supposed to be spurious.

A solution is suggested by a comparison of the two texts. The significant differences consist exclusively of extra material included in the Banno version which is said to be absent from the Kartārpur manuscript. The three most important instances are a hymn by Mīrā Bāī, another by Sūr Dās, and a third by Gurū Arjan. Given this situation one is tempted to conclude that the extra material must originally have been included in the Kartārpur manuscript and then subsequently obliterated. Tact and persuasion having failed to secure access to the Kartārpur volume, I was compelled to fall back on the evidence which existed apart from the actual manuscript. An analysis of this evidence seemed to confirm a theory already tentatively formed.

Two of the basic points have already been noted. First, there is the universal agreement that the important differences distinguishing the Kartārpur manuscript from the Banno version consist exclusively of material included in the latter which is not to be found in the former. Secondly, there is the testimony of those who have inspected the Kartārpur manuscript concerning the obliteration of portions of its text.

A third factor is the presence in the standard printed editions of two fragments, corresponding to two of the three additional Banno hymns. In *Rāmakalī rāg* there occurs a single couplet where there should apparently be a complete hymn.[27] The remainder of the hymns in the same section indicate that the couplet must be either the first two lines of a *chhant*, or a shalok introducing a *chhant*. The second fragment corresponds to the Sūr Dās hymn in *Sāraṅg rāg*. In this instance the standard printed text contains only the first line.[28] There seemed to be only one possible reason for the appearance of these two fragments. The bulk of the hymn in each case must have been

[26] Jodh Singh, op. cit.
[27] *Ādi Granth*, p. 927.
[28] Ibid., p. 1253.

deleted, leaving a small remainder which was faithfully copied into the standard printed text.

A fourth point seemed to clinch the issue. The Banno text of the missing portions indicated good reasons for later deletion, particularly in the case of the *Rāmakalī* hymn by Gurū Arjan. This hymn describes the puberty rites conducted by Gurū Arjan at the initiation of his son Hargobind. The rites follow a standard Hindu pattern and in the third stanza there is a reference to the manner in which the boy's head was shaved.[29] This feature is in obvious contradiction to the later prohibition of hair-cutting. When the prohibition became mandatory, not merely for Jaṭ Sikhs but also those of other castes, the reference in the hymn could only be regarded as intolerable.

Finally, there was ample evidence that others had already formed the same suspicions concerning the Kartārpur manuscript and were seeking alternative explanations. One writer has declared that the present Kartārpur manuscript is a Banno version, adding that the original manuscript of the *Ādi Granth* must have been lost.[30] Another has suggested that the present manuscript must be a first draft, subsequently amended by the Gurū himself.[31] Their evident uneasiness strengthened a hypothesis which already seemed firmly founded.

By this time the hypothesis will have become obvious. The conclusion which seemed to be emerging with increasing assurance was that the widely disseminated Banno version must represent the original text; and that the Kartārpur manuscript must be a shortened version of the same text. A few portions must have been deleted because they could not be reconciled with beliefs subsequently accepted by the Panth. This much appeared to be well established and another point could be added as a possibility. It seemed likely that the amendments had originally been made by omitting the problem passages from later manuscripts rather than by deleting them from the Kartārpur manuscript. These later manuscripts reflected the distinctive pattern of Khālsā belief. The omission of the prob-

[29] India Office Library MS. Panj. F1, f. 462b. British Museum MS. Or. 2159, f. 582a/584a.

[30] Sant Indar Singh Chakarvarti, *Pañjābī Duniān* (Jan.-Feb. 1965), p. 196.

[31] This opinion was advanced orally during the discussion which followed the reading of Dr Loehlin's paper 'A Westerner looks at the Kartarpur Granth' at the first session of the Punjab History Conference. See above, p. 74, n. 21.

lem passages together with the addition of compositions by Gurū Tegh Bahādur constituted the Damdamā version of the *Ādi Granth.* Later still, portions of the Kartārpur manuscript (the original manuscript written by Bhāī Gurdās) were rather ineptly obliterated in order to bring the two versions into line.

That, however, was not to be the end of the problem. In 1968 Dr. Jodh Singh published his book *Srī Kartārpurī Bīṛ de Daraśan.* Dr. Jodh Singh was the person who had devoted the closest attention to the manuscript during the period when it was under litigation and had taken the opportunity to make copious notes. These notes form the substance of his book. They raise once again issues which previously had seemed to be satisfactorily settled, and although they do not altogether destroy the thesis based upon the comparison with the extant Banno text, they do deprive it of its earlier assurance.

From these notes it appears that the Mīrā Bāī hymn still fits the original thesis, for Dr. Jodh Singh confirms that it was in the original manuscript.[32] The hymns by Sūr Dās and Gurū Arjan are, however, in doubt. In the case of the former Dr. Jodh Singh reports that the opening line of the hymn (the line which appears in the standard printed text) is followed by four blank lines in the manuscript. This could accommodate the remainder of the hymn, but Dr. Jodh Singh assures us that there has been no obliteration at this point.[33] He reports a similar condition in the case of Gurū Arjan's *Rāmakalī* hymn. The solitary couplet is followed by a blank space which extends to more than two folios—and no obliteration. He also states that although the couplet is in the same hand as the text which precedes it the scribe has used a different pen.[34]

From this report it is clear that the issue should still be regarded as open. The importance of the questions which it raises deserves to be firmly stressed. Whereas the hymns by Mīrā Bāī and Sūr Dās involve interesting textual problems of no great significance, the same certainly cannot be said for the *Rāmakalī* hymn by Gurū Arjan. Did Gurū Arjan write this hymn? If it could be established that he did in fact compose it, the relationship of the later Khālsā discipline to the earlier teachings of the Gurūs could be made dramatically clearer. But

[32] Op. cit., p. 106. [33] Ibid., p. 113. [34] Ibid., p. 97.

did he compose it? Although the unity of the complete hymn as recorded in the Banno version implies the work of one man, the failure of the Kartārpur manuscript to record more than one couplet prevents us from drawing any firm conclusions.

This concludes the description of the *Ādi Granth*, or *Gurū Granth Sāhib*, except to add that there exist some excellent vernacular commentaries on the text of the standard printed edition.[35] The brief remainder of the essay will be devoted to a rapid survey of the other works which can be regarded as Sikh scriptures. It should be emphasized that the brevity of the treatment reflects no estimate of their importance. Although they are not to be compared to the *Ādi Granth* in terms of sanctity or actual use they are nevertheless works of very considerable significance, not least as historical source material.

The first of these supplementary scriptures to be noted is the *Dasam Granth*, or 'Book of the Tenth Gurū'.[36] This work must be distinguished from the Damdamā version of the *Ādi Granth* with which it is sometimes confused. The *Dasam Granth* is a large collection of miscellaneous writings attributed to Gurū Gobind Siṅgh which in no way overlap the contents of the *Ādi Granth*. In marked contrast to the consistent religious message of the earlier collection it embodies a considerable diversity of

[35] The first of the vernacular commentaries was the celebrated *Ādi Srī Gurū Granth Sāhibjī Saṭīk*, commonly known as the *Farīdkoṭ Ṭīkā* because it was commissioned by the Raja of Farīdkoṭ and published in four volumes under his patronage in 1905. A second edition appeared in 1924 and a third was published by the Languages Department, Patiala, in 1970. Its principal contributor was Bhai Badan Singh Giani. The best commentary is the four-volume *Śabadārath Srī Gurū Granth Sāhib Jī* (n.p., 1936–41), largely the work of the late Principal Teja Singh but published anonymously. The complete *Ādi Granth* text is given, with commentary on the facing page. Much fuller but still incomplete is Vir Singh's *Santhyā Srī Gurū Granth Sāhib* (Amritsar, 1958–62). Seven volumes have so far been published and the remainder, though long delayed, are said to be forthcoming. Another excellent work is Professor Sahib Singh's *Srī Gurū Granth Sāhib Darapaṇ*, published in ten volumes (Jullundur, 1962–4). Two supplementary works which are indispensable for a study of the *Ādi Granth* text are *Srī Gurū Granth Koś* (3 vols., Amritsar, 4th ed., 1950) and *Guru Śabad Ratan Prakāś* (Patiala, 1963). The first of these is a dictionary of difficult words occurring in the *Ādi Granth*, published anonymously but known to be largely the work of Vir Singh. The second is a line-index of the *Ādi Granth* compiled by Kaur Singh Nihang and originally published in 1923. To these should be added the noble *Guruśabad Ratanākar Mahān Koś* of Kahn Singh Nabha (Patiala, 2nd ed., 1960), commonly known simply as the *Mahān Koś* and justly claiming to be 'An Encyclopaedia of Sikh Literature'.

[36] A printed edition is available, published by Bhai Jawahar Singh Kirpal Singh, Bazar Mai Sewan, Amritsar. Two studies of the *Dasam Granth* are Dharam Pal Ashta, *Poetry of the Dasam Granth* (New Delhi, 1959), and C. H. Loehlin, *The Granth of Guru Gobind Singh and the Khalsa Brotherhood* (Lucknow, 1971). See also Khushwant Singh, *A History of the Sikhs*, Vol. 1, pp. 313–18.

material, owing a particular debt to the Purāṇas and to anecdotes from current oral tradition.

The contents of the *Dasam Granth* fall into four groups. First, there are two works which may be classified as autobiographical. The *Vichitar Nāṭak* is an account by the Gurū himself of his genealogy, of his previous incarnation as an ascetic in the Himālayas, and of his earlier battles. The *Ẓafar-nāmā* is a defiant epistle addressed to the Mughal emperor Aurangzeb.

Secondly, there are four compositions expressing the militant piety which characterizes the tenth Gurū. These are the *Jāp* (a work of great influence which must be distinguished from the *Japjī* of Nānak), the *Akāl Ustat*, the *Giān Prabodh*, and the *Śabad Hazāre*.

Thirdly, there are two miscellaneous works. These are the *Savaiyye* or 'Panegyrics'; and the *Śastar Nām-mālā*, or 'Inventory of Weapons'.

Fourthly, there are the lengthy portions relating legend and anecdote—the *Chaṇḍī Charitr*, *Chaṇḍī kī Vār*, the *Chaubīs Avatār*, and the *Trīā Charitr*. As these titles indicate the Mother Goddess Chaṇḍī figures prominently. Of the *avatārs* Kriṣṇa receives by far the greatest attention. The *Trīā Charitr* are tales of the wiles of women which have, with a certain aptness, been dubbed 'barrack-room ballads'.

These four groups differ considerably in terms of length as well as subject-matter and the differences are of significance in any attempt to define the true nature of the *Dasam Granth* collection. The two autobiographical works cover a total of 73 pages in the standard printed edition; the devotional compositions occupy 68 pages; and the miscellaneous works are contained within 96 pages. These three must be set in contrast with the legendary narratives which together account for 1,185 pages. Within this fourth group the *Kriṣaṇ Avatār* covers 316 pages and the *Trīā Charitr* 580 pages.

Were all these compositions the work of Gurū Gobind Siṅgh? The autobiographical and devotional compositions may well be the Gurū's own work, and perhaps also *Chaṇḍī kī Vār*. The remainder must be substantially, and probably entirely, the works of others who were present at his court. The various works were collected after his death (perhaps, as the tradition claims, by the celebrated disciple Manī Siṅgh) and because they had all come from the tenth Gurū's court the ordinal *dasam* was attached to the volume. The language is predominantly Braj, with some Persian, Pañjābī, and Kharī Bolī. As an expression of the Śivāliks' impact upon the Jaṭ culture of the Pañjāb plains the *Dasam Granth* is a historical source of critical importance for any analysis of the evolution of the Sikh Panth. It has yet to receive the close attention which it deserves.

Another anthology which may be regarded as a supplementary scripture is the collection of *Vārs* by Bhāī Gurdās,[37] a writer to whom we have already referred as the amanuensis of Gurū Arjan. A *vār* is, strictly, a heroic ode or ballad, but in Bhāī Gurdās's hands the form has been turned to a much more general use. In his thirty-nine Pañjābī *Vārs* he covers an extensive range of Sikh belief, history, and biography.[38] These compositions are renowned in Sikh tradition as 'the key to the *Gurū Granth Sāhib*' and as such are approved for recitation in gurdwaras. In spite of their extensive use they too have yet to receive from historians and philologists the attention which they warrant. The same can also be said of his 556 *Kabitts* which, because they are in a somewhat difficult Braj, have been largely ignored even within the Panth.[39]

A status similar to the *Vārs* of Bhāī Gurdās is accorded the Persian and Pañjābī works of Nand Lāl Goyā, and here too we must note not only their importance but also their neglect.[40] Although Nand Lāl was one of the poets at the court of Gurū Gobind Siṅgh, it is appropriate that his work should have been omitted from the *Dasam Granth.* Unlike most of the Gurū's other poets Nand Lāl betrays a dominant interest in philosophical issues.

Finally, there are the janam-sākhīs which, because they are so commonly read within the precincts of gurdwaras, may be regarded as semi-canonical. As a complete essay has already been devoted to this body of literature no further description will be offered at this point.

[37] The standard edition is *Vārān Bhāī Gurdās*, ed. Hazara Singh and Vir Singh (Amritsar: the Khalsa Samachar, 7th ed., 1962).

[38] The extant collection consists of forty *vārs*. There is, however, no doubt that the last of these is by a later hand.

[39] *Kabbit Bhāī Gurdās*, ed. Vir Singh (Amritsar: the Khalsa Samachar, 3rd ed., 1966).

[40] *Kulliyāt-i-Bhāī Nand Lāl Goyā*, ed. Ganda Singh (Malacca: Sikh Sangat, 1963).

The world is poorer for its ignorance of the Sikh scriptures. Although it is doubtless true that translations can rarely recapture the charm of a choice original, it is equally true that competence is always attainable and that a skilled translator who senses the power of the original Pañjābī will occasionally reproduce its spirit and beauty as well as its literal meaning. Already there are promising beginnings. We must hope that they prosper.

5

CASTE IN THE SIKH PANTH

IT was during the last two decades of the eighteenth century that the Sikhs first became a subject of interest to British observers. Although the primary interest of the British was, predictably, in the military and political strength of the Sikh misls currently controlling the Pañjāb, the accounts which derive from this period also attempt to describe the rudiments of Sikh religion and society.[1]

Two comments relating to the caste constituency of the Panth recur in these accounts and in their early nineteenth-century successors. The first is that it consists 'mostly of the *Jaut* [Jaṭ] tribe'.[2] This 'tribe' is, however, generally recognized as the bulk and dominant nucleus of the Panth, not as its exclusive membership. Other castes were perceived within the Khālsā brotherhood and it was this mingling of castes which prompted the second recurring comment:

> The Article indeed of receiving Proselytes, in the Doctrine of the Seicks causes an essential deviation from the Hindoo system. It totally overthrows those wonderful Barriers which were constructed and affixed by Brimha [Brahma, *sic* Manu], for the arrangement of the different ranks and professions of his People.[3]

Caste distinctions were, in other words, obliterated within the eighteenth-century Panth.

Although the first of these observations can be accepted, the second must be substantially qualified. Another Englishman of the same period observed one major qualification clearly and dimly perceived another. Writing in 1803 William Francklin commented:

[1] These narratives have been edited by Ganda Singh and published in *Indian Studies: Past and Present*, Vol. 2, nos. 3 and 4; and Vol. 3, no. 2. *Indian Studies: Past and Present* subsequently published them collectively under the title *Early European Accounts of the Sikhs*, ed. Ganda Singh (Calcutta, 1962).

[2] James Browne, *History of the Origin and Progress of the Sicks* (1783). Ganda Singh, op. cit., p. 13. Also ibid., pp. 56, 105.

[3] Letter from George Forster to Mr. Gregory at Lucknow, dated in Kachmer 1783, Ganda Singh, p. 79. Also ibid., pp. 18, 56, 92.

> The Seiks allow foreigners of every description to join their standard, to sit in their company, and to shave their beards, but excepting in the instance of the Jauts, they will not consent to intermarriages, nor will they eat or drink from the hands of an alien except he be a Bramin, and for this cast they always profess the highest veneration.[4]

The qualification which Francklin plainly marked was a restriction on commensality, overtly expressed in a continuing respect for Brāhmaṇ services. Pañjābī sources of the same period confirm the strength of this attitude.[5] Francklin also draws attention to a restriction on intermarriage. Although his reference concerns foreigners it seems clear that the comment should properly be applied to conventions observed within the Panth. This, at least, is the conclusion implied by nineteenth- and twentieth-century observations. These later observations reveal an insistent regard for marriage alliances along conventional lines, qualified only by a limited measure of freedom in the case of the Jaṭs. Entry to the Panth was open to all and within it caste was certainly discounted. It was, however, by no means obliterated. It survived in terms of commensality and marriage patterns, demonstrating in both respects that degree of tenacity which has proved so puzzling to successive generations of foreigners.

The comments by early British writers serve to introduce the important question of caste in the Sikh Panth. There are, in fact, two issues which warrant our attention. The first is the comparatively simple empirical question of the actual caste constituency of the Panth. This particular issue has already obtruded in the numerous references to Jaṭ dominance which appear in the earlier essays. The second question concerns the survival of caste observance within the Panth, a feature which for many Sikhs constitutes a continuing moral problem. On the one hand there are the egalitarian traditions inherited from the teachings of the Gurūs; and on the other one is confronted by the undeniable persistence of caste. There are thus separate issues of constituency and of attitude. They are, however, intimately related and it will accordingly be convenient to treat them concurrently.

[4] William Francklin, *Military Memoirs of Mr George Thomas*, Ganda Singh, p. 105.

[5] Chopā Singh, 'Rahit-nāmā', unpub. MS. no. 6124 of the Sikh Reference Library, Amritsar, f. 6a.

At first sight there seems to be no problem as far as the teachings of the Gurūs are concerned. Gurū Nānak declared his attitude in a famous and oft-repeated couplet:

phakaṛ jātī phakaṛ nāu
sabhanā jīā ikā chhāu

Worthless is caste and worthless an exalted name.
For all mankind there is but a single refuge.[6]

This is merely the most famous of his numerous pronouncements on this particular subject. Many more can be added.

Observe the divine light in a man and ask not his caste
For there is no caste in the hereafter[7]

Sacrifice, oblation, the reading of sacred texts—
all are futile.
Only that which pleases Thee is acceptable in
Thy sight.
Kingship, possessions, beauty, and riches—all
are but transient clouds,
And when the Sun's chariot ascends the true
landscape comes into view.
In the hereafter name and caste count for nothing.[8]

It was the quest for salvation which above all else concerned Nānak and in this quest caste status provided no assistance to the individual. It was, in fact, a positive hindrance for many in that it nurtured a detrimental pride. The way to God was through holy living, not through any accident of birth nor through the observance of any external ritual.

Nānak's successors repeat this same message both by precept and by the institution of distinctive customs.

When you die you do not carry your caste with you.
It is your deeds [and not your caste] which will
determine your fate.[9]

These are the words of Gurū Amar Dās and he, it seems, was

[6] *Vār Sirī Rāgu* 3:1, *Ādi Granth* (*AG*), p. 83.
[7] *Āsā* 3, *AG*, p. 349.
[8] *Malār* 8, *AG*, p. 1257: For other examples of Gurū Nānak's pronouncements on caste see *Vār Mājh* 10, *AG*, p. 142; *Vār Āsā* 11:3, *AG*, p. 469; *Sāraṅg* 3, *AG*, p. 198; *Prabhātī* 10, *AG*, p. 1330.
[9] *Āsā* 8, *AG*, p. 363.

the Gurū responsible for borrowing from the Sūfīs the practice of compulsory commensality.[10] To this day every Sikh gurdwara must have attached to it a dining-room (the *laṅgar*) in which meals are served to any who may care to accept them. This strikes at the very heart of an important aspect of caste and there can be no doubt that the practice was instituted for this very reason.

The words of the fourth Gurū, Rām Dās, carry forward the same message.

> There are four castes and four traditional stages in
> the holy life.
> But he who meditates on God he it is who is supreme.[11]

The fifth Gurū, Arjan, repeats it yet again and significantly includes in the scripture which he prepared the works of two earlier poets who had made the same point with even greater force. Kabīr, a low-caste weaver (*julāhā*), and Ravidās, an outcaste leather-worker (*chamār*), had both insisted in their devotional poetry that the way of salvation was as open to them as to anyone else. Gurū Arjan indicated his agreement by retaining their hymns in the *Granth Sāhib*, the sacred scripture of the Sikhs. Also included were works attributed to Nāmdev, a low-caste calico printer (*chhīmbā*).

Finally, and most significant of all, there was the example set by Gurū Gobind Siṅgh at the institution of the Khālsā brotherhood in 1699, specifically in the ceremony of initiation which he is said to have introduced on that occasion.[12] The climax of this ceremony was a form of baptism which required all candidates to drink from a common bowl, striking once again at the notion of ritual purity. In Sikh tradition the anti-caste quality of the Khālsā initiation is further strengthened by the belief that the first five to accept baptism included a representative range from high-caste Khatrī through middle-caste Jaṭ to low-caste barber and washerman.

The baptismal procedure of the Khālsā was strengthened and confirmed in the post-initiation experience of its members by the custom of presenting sacramental food (*kaṛāh praśād*)

[10] W. H. McLeod, *Gurū Nānak and the Sikh Religion* (Oxford, 1968), p. 210.
[11] *Goṇḍ* 4, *AG*, p. 861.
[12] See above, p. 15.

before copies of the scripture installed in gurdwaras. The significance of this rite lies not merely in the actual presentation, but also in the subsequent consumption of the food. Having been brought into a gurdwara by Sikhs of any caste the individual offerings of *kaṛāh praśād* are deposited in a single dish and a portion is distributed amongst all who are present in the congregation. All are expected to accept a share, regardless of their own caste or of the sources of the offering. This ensures that high castes consume food received in effect from the hands of lower castes or even outcastes and that they do so from a common dish. Although the actual period of introduction into Sikh usage is unknown a reference in the works of Bhāī Gurdās suggests that the custom (or something resembling it) was observed at least as early as the time of the fifth Gurū.[13] Those who wish to avoid receiving *kaṛāh praśād* from hands of inferior status can in practice do so, but the intention of the rite remains clear.[14]

And so it would appear that the Sikh Gurūs were, beyond all doubt, vigorous and practical denunciators of caste. From this it would seem to follow that continued evidence of caste distinction within the Sikh community must represent flagrant violations of the Gurūs' explicit commands. It is at this point that some critics of Sikh claims have introduced a suggestion which to Sikh ears must sound grossly impertinent. According to these critics the most prominent violators of the anti-caste commandments are the Gurūs themselves. Nothing rouses a Sikh to greater fury than a censure (direct or implied) of the Gurūs and it is presumably for this reason that the suggestion has rarely found its way into print. It is, however, uttered often enough in conversation and ought therefore to be brought into the open for examination.

The ten Gurūs were all Khatrīs by caste. In other words, they all belonged to a mercantile caste, claiming (as its name indicates) the elevated rank of Kshatriya and commanding a high status rating in Pañjābī society. This is widely regarded as

[13] *Vār* 1:36. Hazara Singh and Vir Singh (eds.), *Vārān Bhāī Gurdās* (Amritsar, 1962), p. 32.

[14] *Kaṛāh praśād* is prepared by boiling equal parts of coarsely refined wheat flour, clarified butter (*ghī*), and sugar in an iron pan (*kaṛāh*). For a more detailed description see Jogendra Singh, *Sikh Ceremonies* (Bombay, 1941), pp. 95–6; and Parkash Singh, *The Sikh Gurus and the Temple of Bread* (Amritsar, 1964), pp. 106–10.

a great pity, even within Sikh society where the numerically preponderant Jaṭs commonly bewail the fact that there was never a single Jaṭ Gurū. It is not, however, the point and substance of the impertinent suggestion. The suggestion concerns the marriage practices observed by the Gurūs. All, without exception, arranged marriages for their children in strict accordance with traditional caste prescription. There is no instance of a Gurū having contracted on behalf of his children marriages with boys or girls from lower castes (nor indeed from a higher rank, although in view of the elevated Khatrī status this is less significant). All the Gurūs, themselves Khatrīs, married Khatrī wives and this, declare their critics, is the true measure of their sincerity. How can one respect a commandment when its promulgators ignore it?

There are two answers which can be offered to this unpublished and unnecessarily embarrassing dilemma. The first is that the Gurūs were not concerned with the institution of caste as such, merely with the belief that it possesses soteriological significance. Caste can remain, but not the doctrine that one's access to salvation depends upon one's caste ranking. The way of salvation is open to all regardless of caste. Stripped of its religious content it can retain the status of a harmless social convention.

This deprives caste of some of its meaning, but by no means all. Was this what the Gurūs meant? Although their utterances (notably the stress upon there being no caste *in the hereafter*) might suggest this, their institutions (commensality in the *laṅgar*, distribution of *kaṛāh praśād* in the gurdwara, and baptism from a common bowl) indicate that they intended their denunciation of caste to be carried significantly further. A reasonable conclusion appears to be that whereas they were vigorously opposed to the *vertical* distinctions of caste they were content to accept it in terms of its *horizontal* linkages. This constitutes our second answer to the suggestion of inconsistency on the part of the Gurūs.

Whereas the first of these rebuttals is easily comprehended the second requires a brief explanation if the attitude of the Gurūs is to be fully understood. This is particularly necessary in the case of non-Indian readers who, having been nurtured on the concept of a traditional fourfold caste hierarchy, persistently apply this classical model to all areas of Indian society. Outside India caste is commonly understood as a single and generally uniform hierarchical 'system'. At the apex of the pyramid sits the Brāhmaṇ, or 'priest'. Below him we find the Kshatriya, or 'warrior'; then the Vaishya, or mercantile caste; and finally the Shudra, incorporating cultivators and such menials as possessed caste ranking. Below the pyramid we find the 'outcastes', notably the sweepers and leather-workers.

It is this classical hierarchy of four *varṇas* (literally 'colours') which is popularly supposed to constitute the 'caste system'. The classical *varṇa* theory certainly possesses a substantial importance as an ideal and in most parts of India the actual status of the two extremes (Brāhmaṇ and outcaste) generally corresponds to their theoretical status. In practice, however, there is no single pattern which can be applied to the realities of caste in India. The many and varied caste hierarchies one encounters in contemporary Indian society and for many centuries past have had only a weak reference to the traditional model.

The traditional pyramid provides a most misleading starting-point for any discussion of caste and for this reason we shall set it aside. Instead we shall begin with the two components of the 'system' most meaningful to those within it, namely the *zāt* (Hindī *jāti*) and the *got* (Hindī *gotra*).[15] The *zāt* is the larger grouping, distinguished above all else by the fact that it is endogamous. In the Pañjāb the important *zāts* include the Brāhmaṇs, Khatrīs, Rājpūts, Jaṭs, Aroṛās, Tarkhāns (carpenters), and many more. Each *zāt* is divided into several smaller groups. These are the *gots*, and the *got* (in contradistinction to the wider *zāt*) is exogamous.

As a convenient example we shall take the Khatrī *zāt*, the caste grouping to which all the Gurūs belonged. Gurū Nānak, a Khatrī by *zāt*, belonged to the Bedī *got*. This meant that his parents were required to arrange for him a marriage outside the Bedī *got* but within an approved range of other Khatrī *gots*. The *gots* into which Bedīs may marry include that of the Choṇās and it was to a Choṇā girl that his parents duly betrothed him. The second Gurū, Aṅgad, was a Khatrī of the Trehaṇ *got*, and his successor, Amar Dās, was a Bhallā. Since the Bhallā *got* may intermarry with the Soḍhī *got* it was to a young Soḍhī that

[15] These are North Indian terms. Other regions use different terms.

Amar Dās married his daughter. This young man, Rām Dās, became the fourth Gurū and thereafter the office was hereditary in the line of his male descendants. All married according to the correct *got* prescription.

This pattern still holds for the vast majority of Indian marriages, both in terms of parental arrangement and observance of the approved horizontal linkage. It is important to stress the horizontal nature of this, the most tenacious of all the many aspects of caste. It cuts across confessional boundaries, uniting Hindu and Sikh without hindrance, and imparting to Indian society a stability which Westerners find difficult to comprehend. Many will claim that Indian society would pay a high price for the abandonment of this relationship and the stability which is its consequence. Aliens may call it antiquated conservatism or unwarranted interference with the rights of the individual, but there are still comparatively few Indians who would agree with them and it seems clear that such critics would receive little sympathy from the Sikh Gurūs.

This emphasis upon the primacy of horizontal relationships is a necessary corrective to a popular misunderstanding. It should not suggest, however, that vertical relationships are unimportant. This would be far from the truth. Notwithstanding the importance of horizontal *got* and *zāt* relationships Indian society *is* strongly hierarchical and one can always expect to find the society of a particular area ordered within a distinct pattern of rank and status. While retaining an overriding loyalty to his *zāt* relationship each individual will also be well aware of who stands above and below him, even if his explicit declarations commonly lay claim to a status higher than that suggested by the general consensus.

Having thus sketched in the most general terms an outline of both the horizontal and vertical features of caste we can return to the question posed by the teachings and example of the Gurūs. We can affirm once again their apparent acceptance of the horizontal relationship, an acceptance unmistakably demonstrated by their willingness to observe customary marriage conventions. What they were apparently concerned to deny was the justice of privilege or deprivation based upon notions of status and hierarchy. They were, in other words, opposed to the discriminatory aspects of the vertical relationship while continuing to accept the socially beneficial pattern of horizontal connections.

Bhāī Gurdās, writing in the early sevententh century, communicates the same impression. In his eighth *vār* he surveys the society which he knows, listing its principal categories and affirming a single way of salvation open to all men. The world, he declares, contains an abundance of different castes and the more important of these he enumerates in stanzas 9–12.[16] Their existence is evidently accepted without question, the point being that the differences of caste identity which they acknowledge are of no significance whatsoever in terms of salvation.

It is also to Bhāī Gurdās that we owe an important list of individual Sikhs, beginning with followers of Gurū Nānak and terminating (in Bhāī Gurdās's own period) with those of the sixth Gurū, Hargobind.[17] In most cases the caste name is given and we are thus provided with important evidence concerning the constituency of Panth during its first century. Three facts emerge clearly. The first is the point already indicated, namely that there is no evident attempt to conceal the caste origins of individual Sikhs. The second is that the early Panth incorporated a broad spectrum of castes, one which is much more diverse than the constituency observed from the late eighteenth century onwards. One particular caste does, however, emerge in notable prominence, and this feature provides the third significant fact. Of those who are identified in caste terms an absolute majority are Khatrīs, the *zāt* to which the Gurūs belonged. It seems clear from Bhāī Gurdās's evidence that Khatrī leadership within the early Panth must have extended well beyond the actual line of Gurūs.

The evidence provided by Bhāī Gurdās can, however, be supplemented by another source. It has already been claimed that the Jaṭ component must have been substantial by the early seventeenth century. This is no mere surmise. It is the testimony of the author of the *Dabistān-i-Mazāhib*, a contemporary of the sixth Gurū and an interested observer of his following.[18] From these two sources it seems reasonable to conclude that during the early seventeenth century Khatrīs enjoyed

[16] Hazara Singh and Vir Singh, op. cit., pp. 139–41.

[17] *Vār* 11. 13–31. Ibid., pp. 193–206.

[18] See above, p. 10. See also J. S. Grewal, *From Guru Nanak to Maharaja Ranjit Singh* (Amritsar, 1972), p. 43.

a particular prominence within the diverse following which constituted the Panth, but that a share of the leadership was also entrusted to individual Jaṭ members. This measure of authority presumably reflected the numerical importance of Jaṭs within the Panth.

During the course of the seventeenth and eighteenth centuries this numerical importance greatly increased, eventually producing the condition of strong Jaṭ predominance noted by the early European observers. An increase in Jaṭ authority matched their preponderance in members. Two processes evidently account for this late eighteenth-century situation. The obvious one is the accession of Jaṭs to the Khālsā. Less obvious was the failure of other castes (notably the Khatrīs) to join it in numbers corresponding to their position within the earlier Nānak-panth. Many non-Jaṭs appear to have preserved their connection with the Nānak-panth without accepting initiation into the Khālsā. This, at least, is the conclusion indicated by the emergence of non-Khālsā Sikhs in the early British censuses and supported by the content of the eighteenth-century *B40* janam-sākhī.[19]

Amongst these Nānak-panthī Sikhs Khatrīs are prominent and Jaṭs absent. The difference is presumably to be explained, in part at least, by the levelling implications of the Khālsā initiation rite, a feature which would offer a serious deterrent to Brāhmaṇs as well as Khatrīs. The Brāhmaṇ Sikh is hereafter a rare phenomenon. Khatrīs would at least retain a loyalty on the basis of their connection with the Gurūs. Together with a small number of other non-Khālsā Sikhs these unbaptized Khatrīs provide a direct link between the early pre-Khālsā Nānak-panth and the so-called Sahaj-dhārī Sikhs of the twentieth century.[20]

Throughout this intermediate period, extending through to the late nineteenth century, the general configuration of the Khālsā constituency seems clear. Jaṭs predominate, a few distinguished Khatrīs appear within its membership and service,

[19] W. H. McLeod, *Early Sikh Tradition* (in preparation).

[20] The *sahaj-dhārī* Sikhs are those who affirm an allegiance to the teachings of the Gurūs without becoming baptized members of the Khālsā (*amrit-dhārī*). The word *sahaj* is normally construed as 'slowly' and the compound as 'gradual-adopters', viz. those who are moving towards a full membership for which they are not yet worthy. A more likely etymology derives from Gurū Nānak's frequent usage of *sahaj* as a description of the spiritual ecstasy which climaxes the devotional practice of *nām simran*. W. H. McLeod, *Gurū Nānak and the Sikh Religion*, pp. 224–5.

and a sprinkling of other castes (all of them 'low-born')[21] can be discerned. The precise proportions are, however, far from clear. It is only with the 1881 Census that the curtain lifts and a degree of precision at last becomes possible.

The 1881 Census returns, while indicating a measure of exaggeration in earlier estimates of Jaṭ preponderance, nevertheless confirmed that this preponderance was indeed a fact. Of the 1,706,909 persons returned as Sikhs (viz. Khālsā Sikhs) 66 per cent proved to be Jaṭs. The second-largest constituent, however, came as a surprise to the British officials who conducted the census. From the Jaṭ total there was a spectacular drop to the next group who turned out to be the Tarkhāns (the carpenter caste) with 6·5 per cent. 'The [numerically] high place which the Tarkhans or carpenters occupy among the Sikhs . . . is very curious', commented Ibbetson in his report on the census.[22] Next came two outcaste groups, the Chamārs with 5·6 per cent and the Chūhṛās with 2·6 per cent. The Khatrīs proved to be sixth-largest with a mere 2·2 per cent. Slightly ahead of them with 2·3 per cent were the Aroṛās, a mercantile caste closely associated with the Khatrīs but ranking lower in terms of status. Twenty other castes produced Sikh returns, but of these only five managed to exceed 1 per cent of the Sikh total. These were the agrarian Kambohs with 1·7 per cent; the Lohārs (blacksmiths) with 1·4 per cent; the Jhīnwars (potters and water-carriers) and Nāīs (barbers) each with 1·2 per cent; and the Rājpūts with 1·1 per cent. The Chhīmbās (calico-printers) were returned as exactly 1 per cent.[23]

Although the 1881 Census certainly had its ragged edges subsequent returns have demonstrated that its analysis of the Panth's caste constituency was essentially correct. Two of the castes listed above (the Jhīnwars and the Rājpūts) can be ignored as their contribution to the Panth has been negligible. This leaves us with two agrarian castes (Jaṭ and Kamboh); two mercantile castes (Khatrī and Aroṛā); four artisan castes (Tarkhān, Lohār, Nāī, and Chhīmbā); and two outcaste groups (Chamār and Chūhṛā). To these we should add one smaller caste with a particularly interesting history within the modern

[21] Irfan Habib, *The Agrarian System of Mughal India* (London, 1963), p. 345.
[22] *Census of India 1881*, Vol. 1, Book 1 (Lahore, 1883), p. 108.
[23] Ibid., p. 107.

Panth. This is the Kalāl or distiller *zāt*, the Sikh members of which style themselves Āhlūwāliās. These eleven remain the principal constituents of the Panth.

A general comment which should precede the individual descriptions of the more important of these groups concerns the progressive increase in over-all Sikh numbers which has been evident ever since the 1881 Census. Whereas the 1881 total amounted to only 1,706,909 (including Delhi) the 1931 figure had risen to 4,071,624 (excluding Delhi).[24] The impact is slightly reduced by the inclusion from 1911 onwards of non-Khālsā Sikhs, but as these totalled only 281,903 in 1931[25] their numbers make comparatively little difference. Two separate processes must be distinguished here. The increment in excess of natural increase was clearly produced in almost all instances by a switch from Hindu to Sikh. This, as the 1931 enumerator pointed out, was to be observed chiefly amongst the agrarian and artisan castes (he should have added the outcastes) and was a response to a belief that enhanced status would result from the change.[26] The Panth still retained its egalitarian appeal and caste returns during the half-century 1881–1931 serve to document this process.[27] It was a process greatly stimulated by the reforming zeal of the Siṅgh Sabhā movement and later by the political concerns of the Akālī Dal. A fundamental aspect of Siṅgh Sabhā policy was recovery of the Gurūs' insistence on equality. In this respect their energies were enlivened by indications that Christian missionaries were managing to convert Sikh outcastes.

The Siṅgh Sabhā was also largely responsible for the second of the processes to be distinguished within the rising Sikh returns. In response to its insistence on Khālsā forms as the only proper observance for Sikhs many who had previously been content with Sahaj-dhārī status were persuaded to accept baptism into the Khālsā. Because the non-Khālsā pattern had been particularly common amongst Khatrīs and (to a lesser degree)

[24] *Census of India 1931*, Vol. 17, Part 1 (Lahore, 1933), p. 304.
[25] Ibid., p. 306.
[26] Ibid., pp. 293, 294.
[27] Caste returns do not appear after 1931. In 1961 Sikhs numbered 7,845,843 over the whole of India. Of these 6,695,099 were in the Pañjāb and Haryānā, 203,916 in Delhi, 557,935 in the adjacent states of Rājasthān and Uttar Pradesh, and the remaining 388,893 in other states. *India: A Reference Annual 1971–72* (New Delhi, 1971), p. 11.

Aroṛās, it was within these *zāts* that the appeal had a particular effect. It did not greatly increase over-all numbers, but it did bring firmly into the Khālsā Panth influential elements who were to affect its future policies significantly. The contribution of Khatrīs to the modern Panth has been far in excess of their numerical strength.

We turn now to individual descriptions, beginning with the Jaṭs.[28] Two vividly contrasting views of the Jaṭ emerge from the literature left by British administrators and from everyday conversation amongst urban Pañjābīs of today. An early expression of what was to become the characteristic British view was provided by Ibbetson in 1883. 'These men are the backbone of the Panjab by character and physique as well as by locality. They are stalwart, sturdy yeomen of great independence, industry, and agricultural skill, and collectively form perhaps the finest peasantry in India.'[29] The words of the civil administrator were endorsed and embellished by the recruiting officer,[30] contributing substantially to the developing British theory of 'martial races'. A contrary view emerges from the unpublished comments of many urban Pañjābīs. From these comments there emerges the impression of an uncouth rustic, hard-working perhaps but distinguished more for his attachment to liquor and feuding than for sophisticated pursuits such as commerce and higher education. It is this innuendo concerning Jaṭs which lies behind the many satirical stories featuring the alleged stupidity of Sikhs.

The second of these views is plainly gross caricature, based one suspects upon a mixture of fear and envy as well as on misunderstanding. The first is much fairer, but represents a somewhat naïve interpretation of Jaṭ attitudes and capacities. However 'sturdy' the Jaṭs may have been in the British experience their society offers much more than agrarian competence and military skills.

There is, nevertheless, truth in the observations of Ibbetson and his successors and its content should be acknowledged be-

[28] For a stimulating analysis of Jaṭ society see J. J. M. Chaudhri (now Pettigrew), 'The Emigration of Sikh Jats from the Punjab to England', *SSRC Report*, Project HR331–I, ed. A. C. Mayer, 1971. See also id., *Robber Noblemen* (London, 1975).

[29] *Census of India 1881*, Vol. 1, Book 1, p. 229.

[30] R. W. Falcon, *Handbook on Sikhs for the Use of Regimental Officers* (Allahabad, 1896), pp. 27–8, 65.

fore attempting to sketch other aspects of Jaṭ society. Agriculture is the traditional occupation of the Jaṭs and their success in this area has been impressive. Jaṭs are prepared to perform tasks which others would consider demeaning and their willingness to experiment with new methods of cultivation is producing handsome dividends at the present time. Their history has added military to agrarian traditions and many Jaṭs have distinguished themselves as soldiers. Military careers have served to relieve pressure on land, a purpose which in recent years has been further served by extensive participation in the transport industry. Distinction has also been won by Jaṭ Sikhs in such sports as hockey and athletics.

To these obvious features of Jaṭ society we must attach others which have attracted less attention. The first is the pronounced rise in status which marks the history of the Sikh Jaṭs over recent centuries. This achievement, already briefly noticed, deserves specific emphasis for the light which it sheds on the realities of caste. Although Jaṭs should, in theory, occupy a low-status ranking their experience as rulers and their dominance in rural Pañjāb have elevated them well above their humble origins. In terms of status no Jaṭ feels inferior or downtrodden.

The status which the Jaṭ Sikh now enjoys does not derive exclusively from economic success as an agriculturalist. It must also be traced, as one would expect, to political skills of a high order. Whatever truth there may be in the claim that Jaṭs show limited respect for formal education there can be none in the suggestion that they are unsophisticated people. Their political predominance in the Pañjāb of today demonstrates its absurdity. For the pursuit of political objectives the Panth serves as a firm base, one which has been skilfully exploited. Control and use of the gurdwaras as a platform and as a source of patronage provide the principal components of this considerable political strength. The chief minister of the Pañjāb does not necessarily have to be a Jaṭ, but it is difficult to imagine one surviving for any length of time without Jaṭ support. Although factional disputes persistently divide Jaṭ politics, effective leadership is never far from the Jaṭ grasp. In recent years this has been most strikingly demonstrated by Partāp Singh Kairon, chief minister from 1955 until 1964. The celebrated Master Tārā Singh was not a Jaṭ (he was a Khatrī), but he was supported by an effective Jaṭ lieutenant in Giānī Kartār Singh and was commonly honoured by the declaration that he possessed 'the heart of a Jaṭ'. When eventually he fell from power in 1962 it was a Jaṭ, Sant Fateh Singh, who overthrew him.

Two other features of Jaṭ society deserve to be noted. The first is the absence of formalized social stratification within the endogamous *zāt*. As with other *zāts* the Jaṭs are divided into numerous *gots* but within the *zāt* there is no recognized order which elevates some above others. Such claims have been made, as for example by the numerically large Gil *got* or more recently by the politically successful Ḍhillons. They are, however, claims which others would dispute.

As far as marriage is concerned Jaṭs follow the customary rules of propinquity which forbid alliances between those of the same *got* (i.e. the father's *got* in each case). Until comparatively recently the mother's *got* would also be excluded and in a few cases barriers survive between *gots* which are traditionally believed to be closely related. A large *got* may possess sub-*gots*, the most notable example being the Brāṛ sub-*got* of the large Sidhū *got*. Brāṛs are accordingly required to marry outside the Sidhū *got*.[31] There exist also prohibitions of varying duration which arise from inter-*got* feuds, an example being the long-standing refusal of Ḍhillons and Bals to intermarry. Jaṭs who migrated from Pakistan in 1947 are commonly regarded as unsuitable by those who have always resided in eastern Pañjāb; and in a few instances a *got* is regarded with suspicion on the grounds that it may not be genuinely Jaṭ.

These prohibitions are all informal and some of them are obviously impermanent. It is also evident that old distinctions based on geographical location are now breaking down. The Sikh Jaṭs have traditionally been divided into three categories corresponding to the geographical areas of Mājhā, Mālwā, and Doābā.[32] Mālwāī Jaṭs have tended to look down on Mājhāils, and both have looked down on Doābīs. This is a tradition well advanced in disintegration, amounting nowadays to little more

[31] The ruling families of Paṭiālā, Nābhā, and Jīnd states were all Sidhū. The ruling family of Farīdkoṭ was Brāṛ.

[32] Respectively (1) the lower plains tract between the Beās and Rāvī rivers, extending westwards beyond the latter for an indeterminate distance; (2) the area south and east of the Satluj river; and (3) the plains tract between the Beās and Satluj rivers.

than a traditional preference. Provided the *got* prescription is observed most will now marry across the old territorial lines.

Finally, we must note the distinctively Jaṭ attitude towards the Panth. Since the migrations of 1947 the Jaṭs of Mājhā, Mālwā, and Doābā have virtually all been Sikhs. Not all, however, are visibly Sikh as the Jaṭ Sikh commonly assumes a considerable freedom with regard to observance of the Khālsā discipline (*rahat*). In his own eyes and those of other Jaṭs he remains a Sikh even if he cuts his beard or smokes tobacco. For other castes it is very different. If a Khatrī shaves he is regarded as a Hindu by others and soon comes to regard himself as one.

It is to the Khatrīs that we now turn. Although Khatrīs claim Kshatriya status (the two terms are cognate) they are in fact a mercantile caste and a distinctively Pañjābī one. Their achievements in recent centuries have been impressive, notwithstanding the comparative smallness of the *zāt*.[33] Commerce has led them to distant parts of India and beyond, and many Khatrīs have distinguished themselves in positions of administrative responsibility.[34] They retain this prominence today. In industry and commerce, government service, higher education, and the professions the Khatrī community continues to demonstrate an enviable skill and many of its members reap substantial rewards. In spite of their mercantile traditions, the claim to Kshatriya status has generally been accepted. Even those who question it must perforce acknowledge that in terms of status the Khatrī occupies an elevated position in Pañjābī society.[35]

Traditional status provides one of the numerous contrasts between Jaṭs and Khatrīs. It is, however, a difference which has shrunk as the Jaṭs have moved upwards. Other differences have proved more stable. Whereas the Jaṭs remain a rural community heavily committed to agriculture, the Khatrīs are essentially urban-based. Many Khatrīs do live in villages, but of these a large proportion have pursued traditional Khatrī occupations (notably money-lending).

Prior to 1947 an important difference could also be observed

[33] The 1931 Census (Vol. 17, Part 2, p. 292) produced a total of 516,207 Khatrīs. Of these 460,851 were Hindus and 55,112, were Sikhs. The small balance were returned as Christians, Muslims, and Jains.

[34] Akbar's minister Ṭodar Mal and Rañjīt Singh's general Harī Singh Nālwā were both Khatrīs.

[35] For an interesting description of Khatrī conventions see Prakash Tandon, *Punjabi Century* (London, 1963), esp. chap. 5.

in terms of geographical distribution. Since comparatively early times Jaṭ Sikhs have been largely concentrated within the plains area of the Mājhā, Mālwā, and Doābā. In this same area the pre-1947 incidence of Sikh Khatrīs was generally light except in the western Mājhā (notably in the cities of Amritsar and Lahore). West and north-west of this area their numbers increased, with a significant concentration appearing in the Poṭhohār territory around Rawalpindi.[36]

Khatrī society also differs from that of the Jaṭs in terms of its internal *got* organization. The Jaṭ *zāt* is, as we have already noted, truly endogamous and generally unstratified, apart from some comparatively minor exceptions. This is not the case with the Khatrī *zāt* which is internally divided into several endogamous units. The principal division is the traditional *chār bārah bavañjah* or *4:12:52* convention. Four *gots* claiming a particularly elevated status observe endogamy;[37] twelve more of intermediate status similarly constitute a separate endogamous grouping; and the remainder (conventionally fifty-two in number) together form a third. Other endogamies have emerged within the latter category, an example being the *gots* of the Sikh Gurūs (Bedī, Trehaṇ, Bhallā, and Soḍhī). The stratification thus generated within traditional Khatrī society is today showing signs of dissolving as increasingly its members form marriage alliances across the *4:12:52* lines. There remains, however, a distinct preference for the old order. Confessional differences are comparatively unimportant with the result that marriages between Hindu and Sikh Khatrī families have always been very common.

Differences between Khatrī and Jaṭ are also plainly evident in terms of their characteristic attitudes towards the Panth and their role within it. Unlike the Jaṭs the Khatrīs have never shown any interest in Sikh identity as a means of enhancing social or ritual status and for this reason a significant degree of Khatrī adherence has been *sahaj-dhārī* (or Nānak-panthī) rather than *amrit-dhārī* (baptized Khālsā). This feature also explains why in contrast to steady increases in Jaṭ membership over the period 1881–1931 Khatrī adherence actually declined during the period 1911–31.[38]

[36] *Census of India 1931*, Vol. 17, Part 2, p. 292.
[37] The four *gots* are Mehrā (or Malhotrā), Kapūr, Khannā, and Seṭh.
[38] *Census of India 1931*, Vol. 17, Part 1, p. 345.

This should not suggest, however, that Khatrī Sikhs characteristically regard their panthic membership with indifference. The reverse is true. Khālsā Khatrī Sikhs are generally punctilious in their observance of the *rahat* and many of them, both baptized and unbaptized, are conscientious in their practice of the *nām simran* devotional discipline. Their services to Sikh theology are unique and reform movements of a congenial nature have received notable support from many individual Khatrīs. Conservative reform stressing education and moral uplift is particularly congenial and Khatrīs have in consequence played major roles in the Niraṅkārī movement,[39] in the Siṅgh Sabhā, and in the surviving offspring of the latter, the Chief Khālsā Diwān. The hurly-burly of Akālī politics has been less to their taste and in this area their contribution has been less prominent.

Other contrasts distinguishing Jaṭs and Khatrīs reflect their basic differences of domicile, vocation, and tradition. Literature provides an example of derivative difference. Amongst Sikh writers, poets, critics, and theologians Khatrīs have been prominent in terms of activity and distinctive in terms of style. It would, however, be altogether false to suggest that visible contrast must necessarily mean deep cleavage or mutual hostility. Cleavages do indeed exist between some Jaṭs and some Khatrīs and there can be no doubt that the term 'Bhāpā' which Jaṭs commonly apply to Khatrīs and Aroṛās from the Poṭhohār area carries with it a perceptible degree of opprobrium. In general, however, the intention of the Gurūs is honoured. Sikhs of all backgrounds still regard the unity of the Panth as a meaningful concept.

One final and minor contrast will serve to link the Khatrīs with the Aroṛās. Whereas Jaṭ Sikhs almost invariably impart a vertical or slightly receding appearance to the apex of their turban, fashionable Khatrīs and Aroṛās commonly tie it in the form of a projecting 'beak'. Many Jaṭ Sikhs (almost certainly a substantial majority) fail to distinguish Khatrīs from Aroṛās, bracketing them in the same *zāt* and sometimes in the same condemnation. The confusion is understandable as their tradi-

[39] Bābā Dayāl (b. 1783), the *sahaj-dhārī* founder of the Niraṅkārī movement for Sikh reform, was a Malhotrā Khatrī. The movement's following has always been largely Khatrī and Aroṛā.

tional occupations are similar and intermarriage between the two is not uncommon nowadays. In terms of both status and occupation, however, the difference should be clear. Aroṛās rank lower than Khatrīs and concentrate on small-scale shop-keeping rather than on the more ambitious forms of industry, trade, or commerce. Most of the Sikhs one sees operating shops in Amritsar or any other Pañjābī city are Aroṛās.

It is not entirely clear when Aroṛās entered the Panth in substantial numbers. Bhāī Gurdās refers to at least two Aroṛā Sikhs in his eleventh *vār*[40] and another, Buhd Siṅgh Aroṛā, emerges as author of the *Risālah-i-Nānakshāh* in the late eighteenth century. Up to this point in time their numbers within the Panth appear sparse, a natural consequence of the Aroṛā concentration in areas beyond the direct influence of the early Panth. It is only with Rañjīt Siṅgh's invasions of Multan and the north-west that their area of major concentration is brought firmly within the Sikh domain, and it accordingly seems likely that the earliest Aroṛā accessions of any numerical significance date from the early nineteenth century. The first evidence they offer of corporate importance within Sikh society is the participation of many Aroṛās in the Niraṅkārī and Nāmdhārī reform movements of the mid-nineteenth century.[41]

British commentators (particularly the recruitment officers) were inexcusably unjust in their treatment of the Aroṛās, branding them as artful and cowardly people quite unsuited to military service. It is ironical that the surrender of the Pakistani forces in Bangladesh at the conclusion of the 1971 war should have been received on behalf of India by Lieutenant-General Jagjīt Singh Aurora. As with the Khatrīs military careers are still unusual for Aroṛās (and acceptable only in the case of direct commissioning). Individuals such as General Aurora do, however, point up the danger of uncritically accepting traditional stereotypes. The Aroṛās have been ill used in this respect.

In the case of artisan and outcaste Sikhs particular interest attaches to the methods used by depressed groups in attempts to raise their status. For all such groups membership of the Khālsā has obviously been regarded as a means of improving

[40] Bisnū Bībṛā (11:19) and Ugavandhā (11:23). The latter reference names another Sikh who may also be an Aroṛā.

[41] Balak Singh (d. 1862), founder of the Nāmdhārī movement, was an Aroṛā.

status. In the case of the Tarkhāns (carpenters) the pursuit of this ambition has taken an unusually interesting form. It can be assumed that many Tarkhāns must have entered the Panth in imitation of the Jaṭ landowners whom they traditionally served in a client relationship. The most famous of all Tarkhān Sikhs had been the misl leader Jassā Siṅgh Rāmgaṛhīā (so called because he had once been responsible for governing the Amritsar fort named Rāmgaṛh). The name Rāmgaṛhīā was taken up by an increasing number of Sikh Tarkhāns from the end of the nineteenth century onwards with the obvious intention of replacing a lowly title with one of acknowledged repute.

Sikh Tarkhāns (as opposed to Hindu Tarkhāns) are now generally known as Rāmgaṛhīās and have attracted to their name Sikhs from a few other artisan castes (Lohār, Rāj, and Nāī).[42] The result has been a new, composite, and distinctively Sikh *zāt*. Rāmgaṛhīā Sikhs have been particularly prominent in East Africa where many went to work in railway construction and funds repatriated to the Pañjāb have helped develop an important complex of Rāmgaṛhīā educational institutions in the town of Phagwāṛā. Many individual Rāmgaṛhīās have secured impressive economic successes by applying their traditional skills to modern needs. The small town of Kartārpur has become a centre of furniture manufacture while small-scale light-engineering industries have been developed in Phagwāṛā and Baṭālā.[43] Other concentrations of Rāmgaṛhīās are to be found in Gorāyā (Jullundur District) and in Ludhiānā.

Outcaste (or Harijan) Sikhs fall into two groups corresponding to their origins. Those who come from a Chūhṛā (sweeper) background are known as Mazhabī Sikhs, whereas those whose forbears were Chamārs (leather-workers) are called Rāmdāsiā Sikhs. One other title occasionally encountered is Raṅghṛetā. This designates Mazhabī families who trace their Sikh connection back to the time of the tenth Gurū. Following the execution of Gurū Tegh Bahādur by command of Aurangzeb a group of Chūhṛās managed to secure his severed head and deliver it for

[42] The Rāj *zāt* is that of the masons and bricklayers. Not all Sikh Nāīs have assumed the Rāmgaṛhīā style and it appears that few if any Chhīmbās have done so. The latter have instead adopted a new name of their own. Sikh Chhīmbās commonly call themselves Ṭaṅk Kshatriyas.

[43] For a fuller description of the Rāmgaṛhīās and also of the Āhlūwālīās see W. H. McLeod, 'Ahluwalias and Ramgarhias: Two Sikh Castes', *South Asia*, no. 4 (Aug. 1974)

honourable cremation to his son, Gurū Gobind Siṅgh. Their descendants subsequently came to be known as Raṅghṛetās, a title now generally superseded by Mazhabī.

A substantial proportion of both Mazhabīs and Rāmdāsiās represent the result of an influx into the Panth during the early decades of the present century, a movement paralleled by similar conversions to Christianity or to a new grouping designated Ād Dharmī.[44] There can be no doubt that the impulse behind this movement was a desire to purge the traditional taint of the outcaste status and that a majority of the converts regarded the egalitarian traditions of the Khālsā as the best hope of achieving this end. It would be false to claim that the hope has been fulfilled. Equally false, however, would be the claim that there has been no gain in status whatsoever.

Three summary points deserve mention before concluding this survey. The first concerns the present caste constituency of the Sikh Panth. Reference has already been made to the multiplicity of local hierarchies which one encounters in any investigation of caste patterns. Two general hierarchies can be discerned in Pañjābī society, one urban and the other rural. Within Sikh society the two intersect without losing their essential clarity. The Sikh component of the urban hierarchy is very small and very distinct, with Khatrīs plainly occupying a superior ranking and Aroṛās close behind. In contrast the rural hierarchy is much larger numerically and rather less clear in terms of order. Three levels are, however, evident. The massive Jaṭ constituency commands the heights. Beneath them and spilling into the urban hierarchy are ranged the Rāmgaṛhīās. At the base, and likewise extending across to the urban section, are the Mazhabīs and Rāmdāsiās.

The second point concerns attitudes and specifically those of foreign observers. Most foreigners regard the Sikh Panth as a generally uniform religious grouping manifesting such characteristics as agrarian skill and martial vigour. As we have seen, the Panth contains within itself a heterogeneous constituency, and many of the features so commonly regarded as

[44] Between the 1901 and 1931 censuses Sikh Chūhṛā returns rose from 21,673 to 169,247; and Sikh Chamār returns from 75,753 to 222,797. *Census of India 1931*, Vol. 17, Part 1, pp. 333, 334. The latter figure is incomplete in each case as many from both groups evidently returned themselves simply as Sikhs in the 1931 Census. Ibid.

typically Sikh should properly be regarded as characteristically Jaṭ.

The final point also concerns attitudes, in this case those of Sikhs themselves. Inevitably the stress in this essay has been placed upon the caste diversity of the Panth and on the fact that notions of status based on caste are by no means extinct within it. This should not conceal the significant degree to which the Panth has succeeded in eliminating many of the discriminatory aspects of caste. The Sikh insistence on equality is far from being a pious myth. Freedom within the Panth may not be a total freedom but it represents an impressive achievement nevertheless and an endeavour which is still proceeding. Sikhs are above all else loyal to the Gurū. The question of equality within the Panth offers no exception to this inflexible rule.

GLOSSARY

Pañjābī forms are given in all instances. Corresponding Hindī or Sanskrit forms are in some instances given in brackets.

Ādi Granth: the *Gurū Granth Sāhib* (q.v.), sacred scripture of the Sikhs.

Āhlūwālīā (*Āhlūvālīā*): the Sikh section of the Kalāl caste (q.v.).

Akālī: 'a devotee of Akāl (the Timeless One, God)'. During the eighteenth and early nineteenth centuries the title designated Sikh warriors noted for their bravery and (during the time of Mahārājā Rañjit Siṅgh) their lack of discipline. In this sense their contemporary modern descendants are the so-called Nihang Sikhs. Early in the twentieth century the title was assumed by Sikhs agitating for freedom of the gurdwaras from private, hereditary control. Today it signifies a member of the Akālī Dal, the dominant political party of the Sikhs.

akhaṇḍ pāṭh: 'unbroken reading'; an uninterrupted reading of the entire contents of the *Ādi Granth* performed by a team of readers.

amrit: lit. 'nectar'; the water used for baptism in the initiation ceremony of the Khālsā (q.v.).

Āratī Sohilā: a selection of hymns from the *Ādi Granth* sung by devout Sikhs immediately before retiring at night, and also at funerals.

Ardās: the Sikh Prayer. See pp. 65–6.

Aroṛā: A mercantile caste of the Pañjāb.

Āsā: a *rāg* (q.v.); one of the sections of the *Ādi Granth.*

āsaṇ: yogic posture; abode of yogīs.

aṣṭapadī: a hymn of eight (occasionally more) stanzas.

avatār: a 'descent'; incarnation of a deity, usually Viṣṇu.

Bābā: 'Father', a term of respect applied to holy men.

bairāgī: Hindu renunciant.

Baisākh (*Vaisākh*): the first month of the Indian year (April/May).

bāṇī (*vāṇī*): speech; the utterances of the Gurūs and *bhagats* (q.v.) recorded in the *Ādi Granth.* The amplified form *gurbāṇī* is commonly used.

bāolī: a large masonry or brick well with steps leading down to the water.

bhagat (*bhakta*): an exponent of *bhagti* (*bhakti*) (q.v.); a devotee.

bhagti (*bhakti*): belief in, and adoration of, a personal God.

Bhāī: 'Brother', a title applied to Sikhs of acknowledged learning and piety. In a somewhat debased sense the term is often used as a synonym for *granthī* (q.v.), *rāgī* (q.v.), or other gurdwara employees.

Bhairau: a *rāg* (q.v.); one of the sections of the *Ādi Granth*.

Chamār: the leather-worker caste.

chaupad: a hymn comprising four short stanzas with refrain.

chhant (*chhand*): lit. poem, song. In the *Ādi Granth* the term designates a hymn of medium length. See p. 71, n. 17.

Chhīmbā: the calico-printer caste. Sikh members of this caste commonly call themselves Ṭank Kshatriyas.

Chūhṛā: the sweeper caste.

Dal Khālsā: the unified army of the Khālsā (q.v.).

Dasam Granth: 'the Book of the Tenth [Gurū]', a collection of writings attributed to Gurū Gobind Siṅgh. See pp. 79–81.

Devī: the goddess Durgā.

dharam (*dharma*): the appropriate moral and religious obligations attached to any particular status in Hindu society.

dharamsālā: in early Sikh usage a room or building used for devotional singing and prayer.

Dīvālī: Festival of Lights, celebrated by Hindus and Sikhs in the lunar month of Kattak (Kārtik, October/November).

Doābā: the plains tract of central Pañjāb bounded by the Beās and Satluj rivers.

Doābī: one who traces his ancestral origins to the Doābā area (q.v.).

Ekādasī: the eleventh day of each half of the lunar month.

faqīr: 'poor man', Muslim renunciant; loosely used to designate Sūfīs and also non-Muslim renunciants.

Gauṛī: a *rāg* (q.v.); one of the sections of the *Ādi Granth*.

ghaṛī: a period of twenty-four minutes.

giānī: one possessing *giān* (*jñāna*, knowledge or wisdom); a reputed Sikh scholar; a Sikh theologian.

got (*gotra*): exogamous caste grouping within the *zāt* (q.v.).

granth: book, volume.

granthī: a 'reader' of the *Gurū Granth Sāhib* (q.v.), the functionary in charge of a gurdwara (q.v.).

Granth Sāhib: the *Gurū Granth Sāhib* (q.v.), the Sikh sacred scripture.

gurdwara (*gurdvārā*, *gurduārā*): Sikh temple.

gurmattā: 'the mind, or intention, of the Gurū'; the will of the eternal Gurū (q.v.) expressed in a formal decision made by a representative assembly of Sikhs; a resolution of the Sarbat Khālsā (q.v.).

Gurmukhī: the script used for writing Pañjābī.

gurū: religious teacher; preceptor. Usually a person but sometimes understood as the divine inner voice. In later Sikh theology the continuing spiritual presence of the eternal Gurū in the *Granth Sāhib* (q.v.) and the *Panth* (q.v.)

Gurū Granth Sāhib: the *Ādi Granth,* sacred scripture of the Sikhs compiled by Gurū Arjan in 1603–4.

Gurū Panth: the presence of the eternal Gurū (q.v.) in an assembly of his followers.

halāl: 'lawful', in accordance with Muslim prescriptions.

Harimandir: 'the Temple of God', the central Sikh shrine in Amritsar commonly known as the Golden Temple.

haṭha-yoga: 'yoga of force', a variety of yoga requiring physical postures and processes of extreme difficulty.

janam-sākhī: traditional narrative, esp. of Gurū Nānak.

Jaṭ (*Jāṭ*): an agrarian caste with strong military traditions, dominant in rural Pañjāb.

jathā: military detachment.

jathedār: commander of a jathā (q.v.). Today the title designates a leader-organizer of the Akālī Dal, the Sikh political party.

kabitt: a poetic metre.

Kalāl: the brewer and distiller caste.

Kamboh: an agrarian caste.

kaṛah praśād: sacramental food dispensed in gurdwaras.

Kaur: lit. 'maiden', 'princess'; the name assumed by all female members of the Khālsā (q.v.). Cf. Siṅgh (q.v.).

Khālsā: the Sikh order, brotherhood, instituted in 1699 by Gurū Gobind Siṅgh.

Khatrī: a mercantile caste, particularly important in the Pañjāb.

kīrtan: the singing of hymns from the *Gurū Granth Sāhib*.

Kshatriya (*kṣatriya*): the second *varṇa* (q.v.); the warrior caste.

lakh (*lākh*): one hundred thousand.

laṅgar: the kitchen attached to every gurdwara from which food is served to all regardless of caste or creed.

Lohār: the blacksmith caste.

Mahalā: a code-word used to distinguish works by different Gurūs in the *Ādi Granth.* Gurū Nānak, as first Gurū, is designated *Mahalā 1* or simply *M1*; the second Gurū, Aṅgad, is designated *Mahalā 2* or *M2*; etc.

mahūā: the tree *Bassia latifolia.* An intoxicating drink can be brewed from its flower.

Mājh: a *rāg* (q.v.); one of the sections of the *Ādi Granth.*

Mājhā, Māñjhā: lit. 'middle'. The area of central Pañjāb lying between the Beās and Rāvī rivers.

Mājhāil: one who traces his ancestral origins to the Mājhā area (q.v.).

Mālwā (*Mālvā*): the plains tract extending south and south-east of the Satluj river, particularly the area occupied by Ferozepore, Ludhiānā, and Paṭiālā districts.

Mālwāī (*Mālvāī*): one who traces his ancestral origins to the Malwa area (q.v.).

mañjī: lit. a small string-bed; areas of jurisdiction designated by Gurū Amar Dās.

masand: holder of a *mañjī* (q.v.); Sikhs appointed from the the time of Gurū Amar Dās onwards to exercise spiritual jurisdiction on behalf of the Gurū in designated geographical areas. During the course of the seventeenth century the masands became increasingly independent and were eventually disowned by Gurū Gobind Siṅgh.

Mazhabī: the Sikh section of the Chūhṛā or sweeper caste.

Mīṇās: the followers of Prithī Chand, eldest son of Gurū Rām Dās and unsuccessful claimant to the succession conferred on his younger brother Arjan.

misl: Sikh military bands of the eighteenth century.

misldār: chieftain of a misl (q.v.).

Nāī: the barber caste.

nām simran: repeating the divine Name of God; meditating on God.

namāz: Muslim prayer, esp. the prescribed daily prayers.

Nānak-panth: followers of Gurū Nānak.

Naqshbandī movement: Muslim revivalist movement introduced into India during the late sixteenth century, vigorously promulgated by Shaikh Ahmad of Sirhind (1564–1624).

Nāth: lit. 'master'. A yogic sect of considerable influence prior to and during the time of the early Sikh Gurūs. Its members, who are also known as Kānphaṭ yogīs, practised haṭha-yoga (q.v.) in order to obtain immortality.

nirguṇa sampradāya: the tradition or sect of those who believe God to be without form or incarnation; the Sant tradition of northern India.

pañj kakke: the 'Five K's', the five external symbols which must be worn by all members of the Khālsā (q.v.), both men and women, so called because all five begin with the initial letter 'k' (*kakkā*). The five symbols are: *keś* (uncut hair), *kaṅghā* (comb), *kirpān* (dagger), *kaṛā* (steel bangle), and *kachh* (a pair of breeches which must not reach below the knees).

panth: lit. path, road. System of religious belief and practice. The form 'Panth' designates the Sikh community. See p. 2.

panthic: (adj.) concerning the Sikh Panth.

patit: 'fallen'; an apostate Sikh, one who having accepted baptism into the Khālsā (q.v.) subsequently violates its code of conduct in some important respect (esp. the ban on cutting hair).

pīr: the head of a Sūfī order; a Sūfī saint.

pothī: volume, tome.

Poṭhohār: the area around Rawalpindi.

Purāṇa: lit. 'Ancient Story', though the *Purāṇas* are in fact comparatively recent and in their present form date from the sixth century A.D. There are eighteen *Purāṇas*. Together they offer a substantial quantity of legend and popular Hindu belief.

Puranic: of, derived from the *Purāṇas* (q.v.).

rāg (*rāga*): melodic organization, a series of five or more notes on which a melody is based. See p. 71, n. 16.

rāgī: a musician employed to sing in a gurdwara.

rahat, rahit: the code of discipline of the Khālsā (q.v.).

rahat-nāmā: a recorded version of the Khālsā code of discipline.

Rāj: the mason and bricklayer caste.

Rāmakalī: a *rāg* (q.v.); a section of the *Ādi Granth.*

Rāmdāsiā: the Sikh section of the Chamār or leather-worker caste.

Rāmgaṛhiā: a Sikh artisan caste, predominantly drawn from the Tarkhān or carpenter caste, but also including Sikhs from the blacksmith, mason, and barber castes.

Sahaj-dhārī: A Sikh who neither accepts baptism into the Khālsā (q.v.) nor observes its code of discipline.

śakti: lit. power. The active power of a male deity personified by his female consort. Cult worshipping the Mother Goddess, consort of Śiva. See p. 13, n. 11.

saṅgat: assembly, religious congregation.

sanyāsī: Hindu renunciant.

Sarbat Khālsā: the 'entire Khālsā'; assemblies of jathedārs (q.v.) and misldārs (q.v.).

sardār: chieftain; leader of a misl (q.v.). 'Sardār' is nowadays used as title of address for all Sikh men. The corresponding title for a Sikh woman is 'Sardāranī'.

sevādār: one who performs *sevā* (service); gurdwara attendant.

shalok (*ślok*): couplet or stanza.

Siṅgh: lit. 'lion'; the name assumed by all male members of the Khālsā (q.v.). Cf. Kaur (q.v.).

Siṅgh Sabhā: the 'Siṅgh Society', a movement comprising several local societies dedicated to religious and educational reform amongst Sikhs. The first Siṅgh Sabhā was founded in Amritsar in 1873.

Sirī Rāg: a *rāg* (q.v.); one of the sections of the *Ādi Granth.*

Sodar Rahirās: a selection of hymns from the *Ādi Granth* sung during the early evening.

Soraṭh: a *rāg* (q.v.); one of the sections of the *Ādi Granth.*

śudhī: 'purification'; a ceremony conducted by the Ārya Samāj to induct or restore to Hindu society those outside its bounds.

Tarkhān: the carpenter caste.

ṭhag: thug; strictly, a member of the cult of ritual murderers who strangled and robbed in the name of the goddess Kālī, but loosely used for any highwayman or violent robber.

tīrath: a sacred place; a place of pilgrimage.

Vaiṣṇava: of, concerning the god Viṣṇu or the sect comprising his worshippers.

vār: a heroic ode of several stanzas; a song of praise; a dirge.

varṇa: a section of the classical caste hierarchy. Four sections enumerated: *brāhmaṇ*, *kṣatriya*, *vaiśya*, and *śudra*.

zāt (*jāti*): endogamous caste grouping.

BIBLIOGRAPHY

AMARJIT SINGH SETHI, *Universal Sikhism*, New Delhi, 1972.

ARCHER, JOHN CLARK, *The Sikhs in relation to Hindus, Moslems, Christians, and Ahmadiyyas*, Princeton, N.J., 1946.

ATTAR SINGH, *The Rayhit Nama of Pralad Rai or the Excellent Conversation of Duswan Padsha and Nand Lal's Rayhit Nama or Rules for the Guidance of the Sikhs in Religious Matters*, Lahore, 1876.

——, *Sakhee Book*, Benares, 1873.

——, *Travels of Guru Tegh Bahadur and Gobind Singh*, Allahabad, 1876.

AVTAR SINGH, *Ethics of the Sikhs*, Patiala, 1970.

BANERJEE, I., *Evolution of the Khalsa*, 2 vols., Calcutta, 1936.

BEDI, K. S., and BAL, S. S. (eds.), *Essays on History, Literature, Art and Culture presented to Dr M. S. Randhawa*, Delhi, 1970.

BINGLEY, A. H., *Sikhs*, Simla, 1899.

BROWNE, JAMES, *India Tracts*, London, 1788.

BURNES, A., *Travels into Bokhara*, 3 vols., London, 1834.

CAMPBELL, GEORGE, *Memoirs of my Indian Career*, 2 vols., London, 1893.

CHAUDHRI [now Pettigrew], J. J. M., 'The Emigration of Sikh Jats from the Punjab to England', in *Social Science Research Council Report*, Project HR 331–1, ed. A. C. Mayer, 1971.

COURT, H. (trans.), *History of the Sikhs*, Lahore, 1888.

CROOKE, W., *The Popular Religion and Folk-lore of Northern India*, Westminster, 1896.

CUNNINGHAM, J. D., *A History of the Sikhs*, London, 1849.

ELLIOT, H. M., *Memoirs on the History, Folk-lore, and Distribution of the Races of the North Western Provinces of India*, 2 vols., London, 1869.

FALCON, R. W., *Handbook on Sikhs for the use of Regimental Officers*, Allahabad, 1896.

FAUJA SINGH BAJWA (ed.), *History of the Punjab*, Patiala, 1972.

——, *Papers on Guru Nanak*, Patiala, 1969.

FORSTER, GEORGE, *A Journey from Bengal to England*, London, 1798.

GANDA SINGH, *Ahmad Shah Durrani*, Bombay, 1959.

——, *Banda Singh Bahadur*, Amritsar, 1935.

——, *Contemporary Sources of Sikh History 1469–1708*, Amritsar, 1938.

——, 'Guru Gobind Singh's Death at Nanded', in *The Sikh Review*, Vol. xx, No. 218, January 1972, pp. 4–47.

—— (ed.), *Early European Accounts of the Sikhs*, Calcutta, 1962.

—— (ed.), *Sources of the Life and Teachings of Guru Nanak*, Patiala, 1969.

GREENLEES, D., *The Gospel of the Guru-Granth Sahib*, Madras, 1952.

GREWAL, J. S., *From Guru Nanak to Maharaja Ranjit Singh*, Amritsar, 1972.
——, *Guru Nanak in History*, Chandigarh, 1969.
GREWAL, J. S., and BAL, S. S., *Guru Gobind Singh*, Chandigarh, 1967.
GUPTA, H. R., *History of the Sikhs*, Vol. 1, Calcutta, 1939; Vols. 2 and 3, Lahore, 1944.
GURBACHAN SINGH TALIB, *Guru Nanak: His Personality and Vision*, Delhi, 1969.
——, *The Impact of Guru Gobind Singh on Indian Society*, Chandigarh, 1966.
HABIB, IRFAN, *The Agrarian System of Mughal India*, London, 1963.
HARBANS SINGH, *Guru Gobind Singh*, Chandigarh, 1966.
——, *Guru Nanak and the Origins of the Sikh Faith*, Bombay, 1969.
——, *The Heritage of the Sikhs*, Bombay, 1964.
IBBETSON, D., *Outlines of Panjab Ethnography*, Calcutta, 1883.
——, *Panjab Castes*, Lahore, 1916.
JODH SINGH, *Some Studies in Sikhism*, Ludhiana, 1953.
JOGENDRA SINGH, *Sikh Ceremonies*, Bombay, 1941.
KAPUR SINGH, *Parasharprasna or the Baisakhi of Guru Gobind Singh*, Jullundur, 1952.
KESSINGER, T. G., *Vilyatpur, 1848–1968*, Berkeley, Calif., 1974.
KHAZAN SINGH, *History and Philosophy of Sikhism*, 2 vols., Lahore, 1914.
KHUSHWANT SINGH, *A History of the Sikhs*, 2 vols., Princeton, N.J., 1963 and 1966.
——, *The Sikhs*, London, 1953.
——(trans.), *Hymns of Guru Nanak*, New Delhi, 1969.
LAKSHMAN SINGH, *Bhagat Lakshman Singh: Autobiography* (ed. Ganda Singh), Calcutta, 1965.
——, *Sikh Martyrs*, Madras, 1923.
LOEHLIN, C. H., *The Granth of Guru Gobind Singh and the Khalsa Brotherhood*, Lucknow, 1971.
——, *The Sikhs and their Book*, Lucknow, 1946.
——, *The Sikhs and their Scriptures*, Lucknow, 1958.
MACAULIFFE, M. A., *The Sikh Religion*, 6 vols., Oxford, 1909.
M'GREGOR, W. L., *The History of the Sikhs*, London, 1846.
MCLEOD, W. H., *Gurū Nānak and the Sikh Religion*, Oxford, 1968.
——, 'The Kukas: a Millenarian Sect of the Punjab' in G. A. Wood and P. S. O'Connor (eds.), *W. P. Morrell: A Tribute*, Dunedin, 1973.
——, 'Sikhism' in A. L. Basham (ed.), *A Cultural History of India*, Oxford, 1975.
MALCOLM, JOHN, *Sketch of the Sikhs*, London, 1812.
MOHAN SINGH UBEROI, *A History of Panjabi Literature 1100–1932*, Amritsar, 1956.

——, *An Introduction to Panjabi Literature*, Amritsar, 1951.

NARAIN SINGH, *Our Heritage*, Amritsar, n.d.

NARANG, GOKUL CHAND, *The Transformation of Sikhism*, Lahore, 1912.

NAYAR, B. R., *Minority Politics in the Punjab*, Princeton, N. J., 1966.

NUR MUHAMMAD, *Jang Namah*, Amritsar, 1939.

PARRY, R. E., *The Sikhs of the Punjab*, London, 1921.

PAYNE, C. H., *A Short History of the Sikhs*, London, 1915.

PETTIGREW, JOYCE, *Robber Noblemen*, London, 1975.

PRINSEP, H. T., *Origin of the Sikh Power in the Punjab and the Political Life of Muha-raja Runjeet Singh*, Calcutta, 1834.

RANBIR SINGH, *The Sikh Way of Life*, New Delhi, 1968.

RAY, NIHARRANJAN, *The Sikh Gurus and the Sikh Society*, Patiala, 1970.

ROSE, H. A. (ed.), *A Glossary of the Tribes and Castes of the Punjab and North-West Frontier Province*, 3 vols., Lahore, Vol. 1 1919, Vol. 2 1911, Vol. 3 1914.

ROSS, DAVID, *The Land of the Five Rivers and Sindh*, London, 1883.

SABERWAL, SATISH, 'Status, Mobility, and Networks in a Punjabi Industrial Town' in Satish Saberwal (ed.), *Beyond the Village: Sociological Explorations*, Simla, 1972.

SCOTT, G. B., *Religion and Short History of the Sikhs 1469–1930*, London, 1930.

SINHA, N. K., *Rise of the Sikh Power*, Calcutta, 1946.

STEINBACH, H., *The Punjaub*, London, 1845.

STULPNAGEL, C. R., *The Sikhs*, Lahore, 1870.

SURINDAR SINGH KOHLI, *A Critical Study of Adi Granth*, New Delhi, 1961.

——, *Outlines of Sikh Thought*, New Delhi, 1966.

TEJA SINGH, *Essays in Sikhism*, Lahore, 1944.

——, *Sikhism: Its Ideals and Institutions*, Calcutta, 1951.

TEJA SINGH and GANDA SINGH, *A Short History of the Sikhs*, Vol. 1, Bombay, 1950.

TEMPLE, R. C., *The Legends of the Panjab*, 3 vols., Bombay, 1884–6.

THORNTON, T. H., *History of the Punjab*, 2 vols., London, 1846.

TRUMPP, ERNEST, *The Adi Granth*, London, 1877.

VAN DEN DUNGEN, P. H. M., 'Changes in Status and Occupation in Nineteenth Century Panjab' in D. A. Low (ed.), *Soundings in Modern South Asian History*, Canberra, 1968.

VAUDEVILLE, CHARLOTTE, *Kabīr*, Vol. 1, Oxford, 1974. Vol. 2 forthcoming.

ANON., *Sikh Sacred Music*, New Delhi, 1967.

Census of India. Census reports for the Pañjāb for the years 1881, 1891, 1901, 1911, 1921, and 1931.

Rehat Maryada: A Guide to the Sikh Way of Life, trans. Kanwaljit Kaur and Indarjit Singh, London, 1971.

Selections from the Sacred Writings of the Sikhs, trans. Trilochan Singh,

Jodh Singh, Kapur Singh, Harkishen Singh, and Khushwant Singh, London, 1960.

Sikhism. Contributions by Fauja Singh, Trilochan Singh, J. P. Singh Uberoi, and Sohan Singh. Patiala, 1969.

Sikhism and Indian Society. Transactions of the Indian Institute of Advanced Study, Vol. 4, Simla, 1967.

The Sikh Religion, a Symposium by M. Macauliffe, H. H. Wilson, Frederic Pincott, and Kahan Singh, Calcutta, 1958.

Aspects of Sikh life in Britain are treated in several of the titles published by the Oxford University Press for the Institute of Race Relations. Of particular interest are:

BEETHAM, D., *Transport and Turbans*, 1970.

DESAI, R., *Indian Immigrants in Britain*, 1963.

JAMES, A. G., *Sikh Children in Britain*, 1974.

Another work concerning Sikh immigrants in Britain is:

AURORA, G. S., *The New Frontiersmen*, Bombay, 1967.

Descriptive bibliographies:

BARRIER, N. G., *The Sikhs and their Literature*, Delhi, 1970.

GANDA SINGH, *A Bibliography of the Punjab*, Patiala, 1966.

——, *A Select Bibliography of the Sikhs and Sikhism*, Amritsar, 1965.

The first of these contains a useful survey of the period 1849–1919.

INDEX

Ādi Dharmī movement, 103
Ādi Granth (*Gurū Granth Sāhib*), 39, 48, 49, 59–79, 81, 86–7, 105
  Banno version, 74–9
  contents, 61, 69–79
  compiled by Gurū Arjan, 20, 53, 60–1, 77, 86
  Damdamā version, 75, 77–8, 79
  different versions, 73–9
  Kartārpur manuscript, 60, 61–2, 74–9
  language, 69–70
  oracular usage, 66, 67–8
  rāgs (*rāgas*), 63, 71
  scriptural Gurū, 16, 17–18, 44, 45, 50, 55–6, 58, 59, 62, 64
  sources, 60–1, 71
  structure, 70–3
  unbroken reading, 68, 105
  vernacular commentaries, 79
  works by *bhagats*, 60–1, 70, 71, 86
  works by Gurū Arjan, 70–2, 76–9
  works by Gurū Nānak, 28, 33, 34, 60, 70–2
Ādi Sākhīs, 24
Afghāns, 15, 17, 46
Āhlūwālīā Sikhs, 94, 102 n, 105
Ahmad Shāh Abdālī, 17, 46, 48, 49
Akālī Dal, 57, 94, 107
Akālī movement, 57, 58, 100, 105
Akālīs (eighteenth century), 48–9, 105
Akāl Ustat, 80
akhaṇḍ pāṭh, 68, 105
Amar Dās, third Gurū, 7–9, 40, 41–2, 44, 60–1, 70, 71, 85–6, 89–90, 108
Ambālā, 13
Amritsar, 42, 48, 53, 60–1, 63, 64, 99, 101, 102, 109
Anandpur Sāhib, 14
Aṅgad, second Gurū, 7, 34, 39, 70, 71, 72, 89, 107
Ārati Sohilā, 32, 105
Ardās (the Sikh Prayer), 63 n, 65–6, 105
Arjan, fifth Gurū, 10, 43, 75, 87
  compiled *Ādi Granth*, 20, 53, 60–1, 74, 86, 107
  death, 3, 12
  view of caste, 86
  works recorded in *Ādi Granth*, 70–2
Aroṛā (mercantile caste), 10, 42, 89, 93, 94–5, 100–1, 103, 105
Ārya Samāj, 67, 109
Āsā rāg, 71, 105
aṣṭapadī, 71, 105
Aurangzeb, 80, 102

B40 janam-sākhī, 24–5, 31–2, 35, 92
Bābur, 33
Bal (Jaṭ *got*), 97
Bālā janam-sākhī tradition, 24, 41
Balak Singh, 101 n
Bandā, 16–17, 19, 44–5, 47
Bangladesh, 101
Banno, Bhāī, 74–5
baptism, 15, 43, 67, 86, 88, 92, 94, 107, 108, 109
Baṭālā, 28, 102
Bedī (Khatrī *got*), 89, 99
bhagat bāṇī, 60–1, 70, 71, 105
Bhāī Gurdās, *see* Gurdās, Bhāī
Bhakti Movement, 6
Bhallā (Khatrī *got*), 89, 99
Bhīkhaṇ, 71
bhog ceremony, 68
Bisnū Bībṛā, 101 n
Brāhmaṇs, 84, 89, 92
Brāhmaṇ Sikhs, 92
Braj language, 70, 81
Brāṛ (Jaṭ sub-*got*), 97
Budh Singh Aroṛā, 101

caste, 9, 11–12, 15, 33, 67–8, 83–104
Census of India 1881, 93
Chamār (leather-worker caste), 86, 93, 102–3, 106, 109
Chaṇḍī, 80
Chaṇḍī Charitr, 80
Chaṇḍīgaṛh, 13, 57
Chaṇḍī kī Vār, 13, 80
Chaubīs Avatār, 80
chaupad, 71, 106
chhant, 71, 106
Chhīmbā (calico-printer caste), 86, 93, 102 n, 106
Chief Khālsā Diwān, 55 n, 100
Choṇā (Khatrī *got*), 89
Christian Church, 67
Christian missionaries, 94
Chūhṛā (sweeper caste), 93, 102–3, 106, 108
commensality, 67, 84, 86, 87, 88
Communist parties, 57
Congress Party, 57

Dabistān-i-Mazāhib, 91
Dakhaṇī Oaṅkār, 71

Dal Khālsā, 17, 45, 106
Damdamā Sāhib, 75
Darbār Sāhib, *see* Golden Temple
Dasam Granth, 48, 59, 60, 63, 79–81, 106
Dayāl, Bābā, 100 n
Delhi, 94
Deva-nāgrī, 70
Devī cult, *see* Śakti cult
Devī, Mother Goddess, 13, 106
dharamsālā, 31–2, 47, 55, 106
Ḍhillon (Jaṭ *got*), 97
Dhīr Mal, 62
Doābā area, 97–8, 99, 106

East Africa, 102

Farīd, Sheikh, 70, 71
Farīdkoṭ ruling family, 79 n, 97 n
Fateh Singh, Sant, 57 n, 97
Five K's (*pañj kakke*), *see* Khālsā, external symbols
Francklin, William, 83–4
funeral ceremony, 42, 66

Gauṛī rāg, 71, 106
Giān Prabodh, 80
Gil (Jaṭ *got*), 97
Gobind Siṅgh, tenth Gurū, 13, 16, 49, 53, 62, 72 n, 75, 81, 102–3, 106, 108
 battles, 4
 confers authority on Khālsā and scripture, 16, 17–18, 44, 51
 death, 16, 39–40, 41, 44, 58, 59
 doctrine of God, 13
 founding of Khālsā, 4, 14–16, 86, 107
 promulgates *rahat*, 15, 51, 52
 view of caste, 15, 86, 88
 works in *Dasam Granth*, 79–81
Goindvāl, 7–9, 42, 61
Goindvāl *bāolī*, 7–8, 105
Goindvāl *pothīs*, 60–1
Golden Temple, 53, 57, 60, 63–4, 67–8, 107. *See also* Harimandir
Gorakhnāth, 6, 22
Gorakhnāthī yogīs, *see* Nāth Panth: yogīs
Gorāyā, 102
got (*gotra*), 89–90, 97, 99, 106
Granth Sāhib, see Ādi Granth
granthī, 65, 105–6
Gurdās, Bhāī, 60, 61, 74, 78, 81, 87, 91, 101
Gurdwara Reform Movement, 56–7
gurdwara (Sikh temple), 25, 47, 55, 56–8, 63–8, 81, 86, 87, 88, 96, 106
gurmattā, 48–50, 56, 58, 106
Gurmukhī script, 57 n, 69, 70, 106
Gurū: Sikh doctrine, 15, 39, 44, 46–50, 55, 58, 59, 62, 64, 66, 67–8, 106
Gurū Granth (scriptural Gurū), 16, 17–18, 44, 45, 50, 55–6, 58, 59, 62, 64, 66, 106
Gurū Granth Sāhib, see Ādi Granth
Gurū Panth (corporate Gurū), 16, 17–18, 32, 44, 45, 46–50, 56, 58, 59, 66, 106–7
Gurus
 personal line, 5 ff, 16, 38–44, 47, 58, 59, 70, 72
 view of caste, 11–12, 15, 84–91, 94, 100, 104
guṭkā, 63

Habib, Irfan, 11
Hāfizābād Janam-sākhī, 31
Hardwar, 9
Hargobind, sixth Gurū, 3, 4, 12–13, 53, 62, 77, 91
Harijan (outcaste) Sikhs, 10, 42, 67–8, 93, 94, 101, 102–3
Harimandir, 60, 62, 107. *See also* Golden Temple
Harī Singh Nālwā, 98 n
Har Rāi, seventh Gurū, 44
Haryānā, 57 n, 94 n
haṭha-yoga, 6, 107, 108
Himālayas, 13, 80
Holkar (Jaswant Rāo), 49

Ibbetson, Denzil, 93, 95
Ibrāhīm, Sheikh, 32–3
India Office Library, 24, 62 n

Jagjīt Singh Aurora, 101
Jahāngīr, 12
Jaijavantī rāg, 71
Jamnā River, 11
janam-sākhīs, 20–36, 40–1, 47, 60, 81, 107
 as cohesive agent, 40–1, 42, 58
 chronological ordering, 23, 24
 exegetical use, 24, 25, 32–5
 function within Panth, 40–1
 hagiographic nature, 21–2, 25–6, 27
 and Hindu/Muslim reconciliation, 28–9
 as historical sources, 25–36
 oral tradition, 22–3
 tales of Nānak, 21–6, 28–36
 various traditions, 24–5, 26
 See also B40, Bālā, Miharbān, and Purātan janam-sākhī traditions; *Ādi Sākhīs*
Japjī, 70, 73, 80
Jāp, 80
Jassā Siṅgh Āhlūwālīā, 18, 46
Jassā Siṅgh Kalāl, *see* Jassā Siṅgh Āhlūwālīā
Jassā Siṅgh Rāmgaṛhīā, 18, 102

Jaṭ (agrarian caste), Jaṭs, 9–14, 18–19, 37,41–5,54–5, 58, 89, 95–100, 102, 107
distinctive customs, 35, 51–52, 77, 81, 84
eighteenth-century warfare, 14, 18–19, 45–6
factions, 37, 45, 96
gots, 97
and Khatrīs, 11, 98–100
marriage conventions, 97–8
martial tradition, 12–14, 18–19, 55, 95–6
origins, 10–11
political strength, 96–7
and Sikh Panth, 9–14, 37, 41, 42–4, 58, 83–4, 86, 88, 91–100, 103–4
status ranking, 86, 96, 103
traditional occupations, 10–11, 95–6
jathās (military detachments), 18, 45–7, 53, 107
jāti, *see zāt*
Jhīnwar (potter and water-carrier caste), 93
Jīnd ruling family, 97 n
Jodh Singh, Bhāī, 76, 78
Julāhā (weaver caste), 86

Kabīr, 6–7, 60 n, 70, 71, 72, 73, 86
Kabīr-granthāvalī, 72
Kabitts of Bhāī Gurdās, 81
kachh(breeches), 15, 51–2, 108
Kalāl (distiller caste), 94, 105, 107
Kaliyug, 33
Kalkā, 13
Kamboh (agrarian caste), 93, 107
kaṅghā (comb), 15, 51–2, 108
Kānphaṭ yogīs, *see* Nāth Panth: yogīs
Kapūr (Khatrī *got*), 99 n
kaṛā (steel bangle), 15, 51–2, 108
kaṛāh praśād, 48–9, 65, 67–8, 86–7, 88, 107
Kartārpur (Dist. Jullundur), 10, 61–2, 102
Kartār Siṅgh, Giānī, 97
keś (uncut hair), 1, 15, 51–2, 108
Khālsā, 4, 14–19, 29, 33, 45–8, 67, 77, 83, 101, 103, 107
code of discipline (*rahat*), 15, 18, 19, 38, 42, 50–3, 54–5, 56, 58, 78, 98, 100, 109
as corporate Gurū, *see Gurū Panth*
destined to rule, 50, 53–4
execrated groups, 43
external symbols, 15, 38, 51–3, 54–5, 57 n, 94–5, 98, 108
foundation, 4, 14–16, 29, 86
hair-cutting ban, 1, 15, 35, 38, 51–2, 77, 84, 98, 108
halāl meat ban, 15, 52
initiation rite, 15, 43, 86, 88, 92, 94, 107, 109
as Sikh Panth, 16, 17–18, 92–5, 100
tobacco ban, 38, 52, 64, 98
See also Panth, Sikh
Khālsā Panth, *see Gurū Panth*, Khālsā and Panth
Khālsā Sarkār, 50
Khārī Bīr, *see Ādi Granth*: Banno version
Khaṛī Bolī, 81
Khatrī (mercantile caste), Khatrīs, 9–11, 89–90, 91–5, 96, 98–101, 107
gots, 99
Gurūs' *zāt*, 9, 11, 87–8, 89–90, 91, 92, 99
and Jaṭs, 11, 98–100
and Sikh Panth, 9–10, 18, 44, 86, 91–5, 99–101
status ranking, 98, 99, 103
traditional occupations, 10, 98, 100
Kīratpur, 13
kirpān (dagger), 15, 51–2, 108
kīrtan, 31–2, 47, 107
Krisaṇ Avatār, 80
Kriṣṇa, 30, 80
Kshatriya, 87, 89, 98, 107
Kurukshetra, 9

Lahaṇā, *see* Aṅgad, second Gurū
Lahore, 12, 16, 30, 53, 75, 99
Lahore court, 62
laṅgar, 57, 86, 88, 107
Lohār (blacksmith caste), 93, 102, 107, 109
Ludhiānā, 102

Macauliffe, M. A., 69, 70, 72
mahalā, 72, 107
Mājh rāg, 71, 107
Mājhā area, 9, 97–8, 99, 107
Malcolm, Sir John, 48–9
Malhotrā (Khatrī *got*), 99 n, 100 n
Mālwā area, 97–8, 99, 107
Māṅgaṭ, 74–5
Manī Siṅgh, 80
mañjī, 42, 108
Mansukh, 34
Marāṭhās, 17, 46
Mardānā, 33
Mārkaṇḍeya Purāṇa, 14
marriage, 42, 66, 68, 84, 88, 89–90, 97–8, 101
masand, 42, 108
mass movement, 67, 103
Mazhabī Sikhs, 102–3, 108
Mecca, 29
Mehrā (Khatrī *got*), 99n
Miharbān, *see* Soḍhī Miharbān
Miharbān Janam-sākhī, 31, 43

Miharbān janam-sākhī tradition, 24, 25, 34
Mīṇā sect, 43, 60, 108
Mīrā Bāī, 76, 78
misls, 17, 18, 19, 45–50, 53, 83, 108, 109
Mohan, Bābā, 61
Mount Sumeru, 22
Mughals,
  and Afghāns, 17, 46
  and Sikh Jaṭs, 12, 45
  and Sikh Panth, 3–4, 12–13, 15, 16–17, 45–6
Mūlā Choṇā, 28
Multān, 11, 101

Nābhā ruling family, 97 n
Nādir Shāh, 17
Nāī (barber caste), 93, 102, 108, 109
Nāmdev, 71, 73, 86
Name (the divine Name), 31, 33, 68, 72
Nāmdhārī movement, 101
naming ceremony, 66–7
nām simran, 92 n, 100, 108
Nānak, first Gurū, 3, 11, 41, 48, 60, 89, 91, 107
  'founder of Sikhism', 3, 5, 38
  giver of salvation, 40
  janam-sākhī image, 21–2, 27–36, 40–1
  life, 5, 21–6, 28, 29
  loyalty of Panth, 38–9, 58
  marriage, 27–8, 88
  myth, 22, 27
  name adopted by successor Gurūs, 39, 71–2
  teachings, 3, 4, 5, 7, 8, 12, 28–9, 33, 43–4, 85
  view of caste, 33, 85, 88
  works recorded in *Ādi Granth*, 28, 33, 60, 70–2, 80
Nānak-panth, 5, 11, 92, 108
Nānak-panthī, 30, 41, 92. *See also* Sahaj-dhārī Sikhs
Nand Lāl Goyā, 60, 81
Naqshbandī movement, 12, 108
Nārāyaṇ, 30
Nāth Panth,
  Nāth Masters, 22
  Nāth legends, 22, 30
  Nāth tradition, 6, 108
  Nāth yogīs, 6, 36, 108
Niraṅkārī movement, 100, 101
nirguṇa sampradāya, *see* Sant tradition

Outcaste Sikhs, *see* Harijan Sikhs

Pakistan, 97
Pānīpat, Battle of, 17
Pañjāb, 2, 4, 5, 9, 10, 11, 12, 13, 16, 17, 20, 22, 26, 27, 30, 35–6, 38, 49, 54, 57, 62, 65, 67, 68, 81, 83, 89, 94 n, 96, 97, 102
Pañjābī language, 25, 69, 70, 81, 82
panth (religious tradition), 2–3, 108
Panth (Sikh Panth), 5, 7–19, 23, 27, 28, 29–34, 37–58, 70, 74, 77, 81, 108
  Aroṛā constituency, 10, 42, 93, 100–1, 103
  artisan caste constituency, 93–4, 101–2, 103
  caste observance, 9, 11–12, 15, 33, 67–8, 83–104
  ceremonies, 15, 42, 43, 66–9, 86–7
  conflict with Afghāns, 15, 17, 46, 48, 52
  conflict with Mughals, 3–4, 12–13, 15, 16–17, 45, 52
  as corporate Gurū, *see Gurū Panth*
  distinctive historiography, 53–4, 56
  doctrine of God, 15
  doctrine of grace, 32–3, 68
  doctrine of the Gurū, 15, 39, 44, 46–50, 55, 58, 59, 62, 64, 66, 67–8
  festivals, 42–5, 106
  heresies, 43
  internal authority, 17–18, 47–50, 55–6, 59, 62–4, 66, 67–8
  Jaṭ constituency, 9–14, 37, 41, 42–4, 51–2, 83–4, 86, 91–100, 103–4
  Khatrī constituency, 9–10, 18, 37, 44, 86, 91–5, 103
  loyalty to Gurūs, 38–41, 44, 87, 104
  martial tradition, 12–14, 103–4
  outcaste constituency, 10, 42, 55, 67–8, 87, 93, 101, 102–3
  political activity, 56–8
  shrines, 7–9, 42, 53, 56–8, 60, 63–4, 107
  worship, 57, 65–6
  See also Khālsā, Sikh
Partāp Siṅgh Kairon, 96
Paṭiālā ruling family, 97 n
patit (apostate), 38, 57 n, 108
Peking, 23
Persian language, 81
Phagwāṛā, 102
Pope, 23
Poṭhohār area, 99, 100, 109
Prem Singh of Hoti, 61
Prithī Chand, 43, 60, 108
Purāṇas, Puranic legends, 22, 30, 80, 109
Purātan janam-sākhī tradition, 24, 25

rāg (*rāga*), 63, 71, 109
Rāg-mālā, 63, 71
rāgī, 65, 106, 109
rahat, *rahit*, *see* Khalsa, code of discipline
rahat-nāmā, 51–2

Rājpūt caste, 89, 93
Rāj (mason caste), 102, 109
Rām (Rāma Chandra), 30
Rāmānand, 71
Rām Dās, fourth Gurū, 40, 42, 43, 61, 70, 71, 86, 90
Rāmdāsiā Sikhs, 102–3, 109
Rāmdāspur, 42
Rāmgaṛh fort, 102
Rāmgaṛhīā Sikhs, 102, 103, 109
Rāmsar, 60
Raṅghṛetā Sikhs, 102–3
Rañjīt Siṅgh, 4, 16, 17, 18, 29, 37, 46, 50, 53, 54, 56, 58, 98 n, 101, 105
Ravidās (Raidās), 71, 86
Rawalpindi, 99
Risālah-i-Nānakshāh, 101
Rome, 23

Śabad Hazāre, 80
Sādhukaṛī, 69
Sahaj-dhārī (non-Khālsā) Sikhs, 47, 92, 94, 99–100, 109
Sahansrām, 61
Saidpur, 33
Sajjan the ṭhag, 31
Śakti cult, 13–14, 109
saṅgats (Sikh religious assemblies), 18, 31–2, 42, 44, 46–8, 109
Sant Bhāṣā, 69
Sant tradition, 5–7, 8, 108
Sanyāsī Panth, 30, 109
sarab-loh (name of God), 13
Sarbat Khālsā,45, 47–9, 58, 107, 109
Śastar Nām-mālā, 80
Satluj River, 62
Savaiyye, 80
Seṭh (Khatrī *got*), 99 n
Shiromaṇī Gurdwara Parbandhak Committee, 56–7, 63, 74
Shudra, 89
Sidh Goṣṭ, 71
Sidhu (Jaṭ *got*), 97
Sikh, Sikhs,
  amrit-dhārī (baptized Sikhs), 92 n, 94–5, 99–100
  definition of Sikh, 37, 92 n
  early British accounts, 20, 83–4, 92
  and Hindus, 3, 9, 28–9, 54, 72, 83, 90, 98
  and Indian Army, 2, 54–5, 95–6
  jokes about Sikhs, 1, 95
  and Muslims, 3, 15, 28–9, 46, 52, 72
  and politics, 2, 56–8, 96–7
  popular view, 1, 103–4
  provincial distribution, 94 n
  sahaj-dhārī (unbaptized Sikhs), 92, 94, 99–100, 109
  and sport, 2, 96
  in United Kingdom, 2, 38, 65
  See also Khālsā, Panth
Sikh comunity, *see* Panth
Sikh Gurdwaras Act (1925), 56, 57
Śimlā, 13
Sind, 11
Siṅgh Sabhā, 55, 56, 58, 62–3, 67–8, 94–5, 100, 109
Sirhind, 13
Sirī Rāg, 71, 109
Śivalik Hills, 13–14, 42, 53, 81
Sodar Rahirās, 32, 109
Soḍhi (Khatrī *got*), 89–90, 99
Soḍhī, Gurūs' family, 40, 44, 61–2, 74, 89–90
Soḍhī Miharbān, 27–8, 30
Soḍhi Sādhū Siṅgh, 62
Srī Hargobindpur, 10
Srī Laṅkā, 34
śudhī ceremony, 67, 109
Sūfī tradition, 6, 35–6, 71, 86, 106, 108
Sukerchakiā misl, 17, 46
Sukhmaṇī, 71
Sūr Dās, 76, 78

Ṭaṅk Kshatriya Sikhs, 102 n, 106
tantric tradition, 6
Tārā Siṅgh, Master, 57 n, 96–7
Tarkhān (carpenter caste), 89, 93, 101–2, 109
Tarn Tāran, 10
Tegh Bahādur, ninth Gurū, 62, 72 n, 75, 78, 102–3
tīrath, 8, 110
Ṭodar Mal, 98 n
Trehaṇ (Khatrī *got*), 89, 99
Trīā Charitr, 80
Trumpp, Ernst, 64
turban, 1, 38, 53, 100

Ugavandhā, 101 n

Vaishya, 89
Vaiṣṇava bhakti, 6, 35
Vaiṣṇava Panth, 30–1
vār, 71, 81, 110
Vārān Bhāī Gurdās, 81, 91, 101
varṇa, 89, 110
Vichitar Nāṭak, 80
Victoria, Queen, 62

Ẓafar-nāmā, 80
zāt (*jāti*), 3 n, 89–90, 97, 99, 110